Praise

An Unimagi...

"*An Unimaginable Act* is a wake-up call to society on a silent epidemic one brave confident woman refuses to stay silent about. Through the trauma and obstacles she has faced in her life, Erin takes readers on a remarkable journey of resilience, faith, courage, and forgiveness. She shares how she turned tragedy into triumph, which has led her on an unstoppable crusade to give children the voice she never had as a child through a very important law that will protect children for generations to come."

—Actress Julianna Margulies

"Erin Merryn: a fearless woman after God's own heart. She has trail blazed the dark territory of child abuse and has brought a healing light to the hurting. Her crusade across America, to mandate child abuse prevention education, is etched on our minds; her spirit and fearlessness awakes and stirs the hearts of all who are touched by her compassion."

—Michael Reagan

"Erin Merryn is a dynamic Christian young lady who shares her tragic testimony of how she was abused growing up, but once she was able to open up, God set her free. She is one of the best speakers we have ever heard and her story will help millions."

—Jim Bob and Michelle Duggar,
parents of TLC's *19 Kids and Counting*

"Erin's Law gives our country the chance to ensure that the children of our nation have the information and tools necessary to recognize and report abuse. Children *need* to be informed about sexual abuse in a structured and safe environment, so that they know there are people who will help keep them safe. My support of Erin's Law stems from my own family's history of sexual abuse and their lack of information on prevention and disclosure. I am proof that prevention is possible, and so I am grateful to Erin Merryn for taking the pain she experienced and turning it in to a national crusade to educate our youth."

—**Mallory Hagan, Miss America 2013**

"Erin embodies the type of courageous leadership needed to address today's social justice issues—not only speaking out on behalf of children suffering abuse, but working to change the law in order to protect future generations for years to come. As a mother, I consider her a role model for my three daughters."

—**Kerry Kennedy**

An Unimaginable Act

An Unimaginable Act

*Overcoming and Preventing Child Abuse
Through Erin's Law*

Erin Merryn, M.S.W.

Health Communications, Inc.
Deerfield Beach, Florida

www.hcibooks.com

The Library of Congress Cataloging-in-Publication Data

Merryn, Erin.
An unimaginable act : overcoming and preventing child abuse through erin's law /
  Erin Merryn.
      pages cm
  ISBN-13: 978-0-7573-1756-9 (pbk.)
  ISBN-10: 0-7573-1756-1 (pbk.)
  ISBN-13: 978-0-7573-1757-6 (epub)
  1. Merryn, Erin.   2. Child sexual abuse.   3. Incest.   4. Sex crimes.   I. Title.
  HV6570.M473 2013
  362.76092—dc23
  [B]
                                                                2013037039

Publisher: Health Communications, Inc.
        3201 S.W. 15th Street
        Deerfield Beach, FL 33442–8190

Cover image © Meredith Jenks
Cover and interior design by Lawna Patterson Oldfield

Contents

Contents

Foreword

Our connection with the world is nothing less than a symphony of brain circuits activated by our senses. Organization of these brain circuits begins before birth and continues well into adulthood. When this organizational process is disrupted, a repair plan is automatically implemented, attempting to slowly reroute critical thinking abilities. Oftentimes, special cognitive testing performed by a psychologist is necessary to reveal clues to a past history of such injury-triggered brain reorganization. Many individuals possess brain networks that are currently compensating for damaged brain circuits. They and their families are also unaware that deep brain rewiring plans had once blossomed early in their lives to correct misfiring brain compartments.

Several years ago, I met an articulate, well-educated young woman who experienced a tonic-clonic seizure, once known as a grand-mal seizure, while driving. She described her story in an engaging and energetic manner, without omitting any details. She casually informed me, almost as if it were not a pertinent part of her story, that she had not had the ability to smell for as long as she could remember. Her neurological examination was completely normal, with the exception of an inability to appreciate odors. As a matter of routine, I ordered a simple electroencephalogram (EEG)—a test where wires are temporarily glued to the scalp and attached to an electronic device that amplifies a difference in electricity between multiple regions of the head. This electricity arises from billions of brain cell connections that constantly generate seemingly random and very small amounts of electricity. These same brain connections are responsible for thought and insight. The EEG is a mapping device. It reveals signals from large groups of brain cells abnormally firing in unison, like a gospel choir bellowing out a refrain. Her test results were consistent with an abnormally functioning landscape in the left temporal lobe of the brain. I recommended a sensitive brain scan to visualize the "lay of the land." Magnetic resonance imaging (MRI) mapped her brain geography. What surprised me most on her scan was the utter lack of a left temporal lobe. This area, which is supposed to be located directly behind each eyeball extending to the area of the ear, is about the size of a medium potato. The left temporal lobe is essential for short-term memory, which allows us to retain words, language, and the ability to write and speak. This region is also critical for smell and taste.

What impressed me most about this clinical encounter was the ability of this talented individual to write and publish well-received books and to speak eloquently, even while addressing large rooms of legislators. She is a true example of resilience.

I explained to Erin that she has temporal lobe epilepsy and should begin a low dose of antiepileptic medication. Upon beginning her medication, Erin actually gained a sense of smell for the first time from as far back as she could remember. A follow-up visit with her family revealed that she had experienced a severe body rash at birth. This rash was likely due to a virus called viral encephalitis, which spread to Erin's brain and went undiagnosed and untreated. She demonstrated clear indicators of this in her delayed developmental milestones throughout early childhood. Erin struggled in grade school and high school. It was not until college that she stood out academically, earning honors and graduating from a master's program. Clearly, her brain reorganized to compensate for the complete loss of her left temporal lobe.

It is impressive that our brains possess a natural tendency to adapt to injury; however, approximately 500,000 people of the nearly 3 million in the United States afflicted with epilepsy lack the ability to reorganize dysfunctional brain regions and respond to medical treatment. Consequently, the recurring seizures that these individuals endure not only interfere with achieving one's long-term goals, but they often impede basic activities of daily living, thus fueling the stigma of epilepsy. Those with epilepsy can be met in every demographic, socioeconomic, and social class in our society. Education, advocacy, and research are the tools that offer knowledge, empowerment, and hope to those struggling to overcome this condition.

Marvin A. Rossi, M.D.
Senior Attending and Director of the Epilepsy SPECT Program
Rush Epilepsy Center, Rush University Medical Group

Acknowledgments

I could not be the person I am today on this mission to protect the innocence of children had it not been for the amazing people in my life who've all played a part in my getting here.

To my parents, who have loved and supported me from the very beginning, thank you for doing the right thing when your daughters broke their silence, showing us the love and care we needed, and helping us to heal. Thank you for being there to help with the challenges I have faced in life, for getting me help when I needed it, comforting me in the midst of panic attacks, staying with me in the hospital, and for always being there to listen. Thank you for believing in me and never doubting me in all that I have ever set out to accomplish in life.

To the two beautiful women to whom I am blessed to call my sisters: We have been through a lot together and have come out stronger because of it. Both of you have helped create wonderful memories from our childhood that I will truly cherish forever. Each moment we are together is filled with so much fun and laughter. You both have been the ones I could turn to in the darkest of times, helping me to get back on my feet again and being that shoulder to cry on when I needed it. Thank you for supporting all that I do in the direction I have taken with my life.

To the man I will spend the rest of my life with: David, you are the best thing that ever happened to me. You showed me how to trust again and that there are good men in this world who will respect you, love you, and not harm you. God blessed me with you. I can't wait to see what life has in store for us together. I love you!

To the therapists in my life who have played such vital roles in my healing—for not only helping me face my past but for talking me through the trauma, comforting me as I cried, creating a safe place to share anything, helping me rebuild trust, giving me healthier ways of coping, helping me work through the anger so that I could let go of the shame, and for helping me find the courage to be a face and voice for others—thank you for helping me pick up the pieces and become whole again.

Thank you to Chief Danny Langloss for taking action after hearing my story and helping me get Erin's Law moving in Illinois. As I often say, good things come from small towns, and they certainly have one in the town of Dixon, Illinois.

To the men and women who served on the Illinois Erin's Law Task Force: for more than ten months, you poured so much of your time, research, and resources into Erin's Law for the state of Illinois that it wouldn't have happened without all of you—thank you!

To my team of legislators in Illinois who believed in Erin's Law and sponsored it, particularly Senator Bivins, Senator Collins, and Representative Mitchell, who were there from the very start, thank you so much for your dedication to Erin's Law. You could have easily passed by this bill, but instead you saw its importance and did the right thing. Thank you for all the work you did at the capital to push this bill through each time and for believing in me. Because of you, we were victorious. I am so grateful for all your hard work on Erin's

Law. Because of you, the children of Illinois will find empowerment through education.

Thank you, Governor Quinn, for believing in Erin's Law and seeing its role in protecting children from sexual abuse. You could have easily signed this bill like it were any other piece of legislation, but you didn't. You put a voice behind it by standing with me in my mission to protect not only the children in Illinois but all children across America. Thank you for giving children a voice.

To all the legislators who have introduced Erin's Law into your state, thank you for seeing the importance in protecting and educating children from sexual abuse. Your time is valuable and the work you do does not go unnoticed. From our time at the capital, testifying to the press conferences and the television and radio interviews, thank you for investing your time in saving children's lives.

Dr. Rossi, I am blessed to have a doctor I can trust. Thank you for all you have done for me over the years in dealing with my epilepsy. You help so many in the work that you do as a doctor. Thank you for fighting for those who face epilepsy day in and day out and being a voice for those who have it.

I am grateful to the staff at *Glamour* magazine. They saw the importance in the work I am doing with Erin's Law and honored me as one of their Women of the Year for 2012. You have helped connect me with so many amazing people who are now helping me in my mission with Erin's Law. Your decision to honor me is going to help save so many children from sexual abuse. Thank you for giving me one of the greatest nights of my life as well.

To Tonya Woodworth, for the countless hours you have poured into editing this book. It has been wonderful getting to know you. As I always say, without editors, authors would not exist. You put the amazing final touches on this book, and I am so glad it got to be you.

To the men and women at Health Communications, Inc., thank you for your support and for believing in me and the work that I do. In allowing me to be a voice against sexual abuse for so many others, you have helped me reach so many survivors, and so many more will be saved through this book.

To Kim Pohl, you have followed me in my mission with Erin's Law from the very beginning. Thank you so much for all your time over the past three years in helping to cover Erin's Law as a reporter for the *Daily Herald*. You wrote so many wonderful articles highlighting my efforts, which have almost always made the front page. Your work has helped me give a face and voice to so many.

Last but not least, to my supporters: So many of you support the work that I am doing through Erin's Law. I read all your letters of support and encouragement. Thank you for believing in what I am doing and seeing the importance in educating children and protecting them from sexual abuse.

Introduction

I n January 1992, just before my seventh birthday, I had gone over to my best friend Ashley's house to play. Ashley and her little brother lived with their single mom. Ashley's uncle lived with them, and he was often left in charge of the children while their mom was at work.

When I arrived, we went to Ashley's bedroom and began playing with her big dollhouse. Ashley eventually left to use the bathroom.

Like a broken film projector reel, the images keep replaying over and over in my mind, hauntingly vivid, as if it just happened yesterday. While Ashley was using the bathroom, her uncle came out of his bedroom and walked into her room. I did not notice him until I heard the door close. Naively, I thought it was Ashley. As I looked up from behind the dollhouse about to say something to her, I saw him standing there.

I was already understandably terrified of this man because of what he had done to me the night I had slept over at Ashley's house the year before. It was something I was reluctant to tell anyone about out of fear that he would come and get me if I told. I was terrified that he would be hiding in my bedroom at night waiting for me.

Ashley's mom was not home, and I was alarmed and uncertain of what he might do. He secured the door, locking Ashley out and me in. I was so scared that I thought I might wet myself. I sat on the floor clutching two dolls in my hands. Her uncle ordered me to get up and onto the bed. I did as he said, afraid of what might happen if I did not obey him. With my eyes drawn to the floor, terrified to look up at him, I walked to the edge of the bed.

I was angry. As my anger turned to terror, I began to cry. He instructed me not to. I was more fearful than before because it was in the middle of the day. The sunlight shone brightly into Ashley's room, heightening my senses and allowing me to anticipate what was to come. I was used to being in darkness, unable to see this man and the terrible things he would do to me. I trembled inside, petrified to look into the eyes of this monster.

As I sat on the edge of the bed with my legs hanging over, he cupped my chin in his hand and lifted my head, forcing me to look up at him. It was as if he wanted to see the fear in my eyes. I believe that by making me look up at him, it was his way of terrorizing me.

He moved quickly, propping my legs up so that my entire body was completely on the bed. He leaned me back in an attempt to take off my jeans. As he did so, I began to fight. I started kicking and screaming, begging him to stop. All my squirming made it quite difficult for him. For a little girl, I put up a real good fight. I was not going down easy. I called out for Ashley. Responding to my cries, I could hear her at her bedroom door trying to get in. She struggled, turning the knob, shaking and rattling it. Then she stopped. I prayed that she was trying to find something to unlock the door. As her uncle pulled my pants down, I heard her messing with the doorknob once again.

Successful at getting my pants down to my knees, Ashley's uncle continued to struggle with me. I was doing everything in my power to keep them on. He had a difficult time, but eventually he prevailed. With my pants around my ankles, he found himself stuck once again, unable to get them around my shoes.

Incidentally, my shoelaces would often come untied, so my dad had taught me how to double-knot them. When Ashley's uncle failed to untie them, he tried yanking off my shoes. But I made it difficult for him, kicking and squirming the entire time. Once he succeeded in getting my shoes off, he told me that if I did not lie still, he would tie my arms to Ashley's bed. It was then that I got really scared and began to cry. He told me that crying was for babies. I feared being tied up and quickly assessed the situation, picturing just how he would accomplish this. His eyes pierced me with a hard, cold gaze. He explained that he would be gentle if I stayed quiet.

I did not know what to call what he put me through that day, but it was definitely not gentle. It was the worst pain of my life. After pulling down his own pants, he laid his entire body on top of mine. With his weight crushing me, I panicked and screamed, "I can't breathe, I can't breathe." He lifted himself up with one hand and placed the other between my legs. I kept trying to squeeze my legs together, but he just kept pushing them apart.

Staring at the ceiling and gripping the bed sheets, I lay terrified while a piercing pain ripped through my entire body. The force of him going inside me felt like a knife ripping me in half. I cried out. Then I began to scream. He placed a hand the size of my entire face over my mouth to silence my screams, warning me to stay quiet. If I did not, he would make it even worse. I could see the sweat streaming down his head as the tears streamed down my cheeks. He groaned and made humming noises. I thought the noises were to block out my crying, but now I know that they were simply the noises of a man getting off as he moved his entire body up and down. When he pulled out, he grabbed my hand and put it on his penis. I didn't pull my hand away. I just held it as he wrapped his hand around mine and moved it up and down.

I stared up at him, but his face was blurry through all of my tears. The whites of his eyes are forever seared into my memory. I cannot get those eyes or his disgusting grin out of my head. I couldn't comprehend why he was smiling at me as I lay there crying. It was so confusing, especially as a child. I was such a fragile, little girl with this extremely large man on top of me. I cried the entire time. It was the worst pain I had ever felt. It is something I will never forget.

The abuse continued as he wrapped his arms around my legs. I tried keeping them together, afraid he was going to hurt me again. He pulled them apart and began having oral sex with me. What I remember distinctly about this was the fact that it didn't hurt like what he had just done. I just remember it feeling very strange. My teeth chattered as if I were cold, but it was really from the fear. I lay there, completely still as he continued to have his way with me.

After having oral sex with me, he spread his legs apart in front of my face and told me to open my mouth in an attempt to force me to perform oral sex on him. I fought back, tossing my head from side to side and clenching down on my teeth, refusing to open my mouth. It angered him immensely. Squeezing my cheeks, in an angry tone he said, "You should have listened." Those words still echo in my mind today.

Suddenly, the weight of his body came crushing down on me again and the piercing pain I had felt earlier ripped through me as he raped me for a second time. I thought I was going to die because I was in so much pain. I began crying hysterically. Gripping the bed sheets, I wondered why nobody heard my screams. Finally, relief came when he pulled himself out of me. I still feared what he would do next and just when I thought it couldn't get any worse, it did.

I thought he was going to let me go when he told me to sit up, but, instead, he ordered me to lie on my tummy. I had no idea what was coming. I stared blankly at the beloved dollhouse that Ashley and I had played with earlier that day. Then I began screaming like I had never screamed before, kicking and swinging my arms as he sodomized me. I honestly thought he was killing me. I was screaming out over and over, "You're hurting me. I don't want to die. I want my mom!" When he finally stopped, he said, "You don't want your mom and dad to know what we do. They won't want you anymore if they find out." Those words haunted me, and I believed him.

I debated whether or not to share these graphic details with you. I have never made them public before because I didn't want to have to go back to that painful place in my mind and watch it play out again and again, knowing just how brutal it was. I decided to put it in God's hands. I prayed, asking him to tell me if I should share these horrific details. A few hours after praying, I went to start my car. When I did, the song "Brave" by Sara Bareilles was on the radio. The lyrics talked about showing how brave you are, saying what needs to be said, and letting the words come out. It was like Sara was speaking right to me when she sang that the silence you have lived in won't do you any good.

After hearing these words, the hairs on my arms stood up. I had never heard this song before, and it could not have been a more perfect answer to my prayers. It was God's way of telling me what to do. God gave me the courage to be brave and let it all out, but it certainly wasn't easy in the least bit. With tears streaming down my face, I typed these painful details as I recalled the most traumatic day of my life. As Maya Angelou once said, "There is no greater agony than bearing an untold story inside you."

After he took what he wanted, he got up, adjusted himself, and pulled my underwear and pants back up. He then warned, "I will come get you if you tell anyone." He opened the door and walked out of the room, acting like nothing had even happened.

I went through unimaginable horror that day. More than twenty years later, I can remember the details as if it were yesterday. That one moment is frozen in my mind. I cannot escape it, nor can I erase that day's events from my mind. I can never forget the sights or sounds of that traumatic day. I remember everything, down to the smallest details: the toys on the floor, the closet doors being ajar, and the words that he said. A few weeks shy of my seventh birthday, I was raped. At such a tender age, I did not know the word, much less what it meant.

As I lay there, it took a few minutes before I was finally able to get up. I was so scared. All I wanted to do was run home. I wondered where Ashley had gone. When I walked out of her bedroom, I saw her sitting outside next to the door, holding the hanger she had been using in a failed attempt to unlock the door. She asked me if I was okay. I told her that I just wanted to go home.

I remember grabbing my purple coat and opening the front door as fast as I could. As I walked down her driveway, I trembled inside. Every step was so painful. As I reached the end of her court and began turning toward my street, Ashley caught up to me. With desperation in her eyes, she caught her breath and said, "My uncle says we cannot tell anyone or else my mom will lose our house."

As I wiped away the tears from my eyes, I assured her that I would not tell. She looked at me with a worried gaze. As if she was not convinced, she said, "You have to pinkie promise you will not tell anyone what he did." I then took her pinkie and locked it with mine, promising again that I would not tell.

It was a long, lonely, and cold walk home. Because I was in so much pain, I struggled to keep my balance. It felt like he was still inside me. I remember every step that I took, the cold air piercing my skin and the tears streaming down my face that eventually landed on the sidewalk. When I got home, I was still trembling and scared.

Once I arrived at my house, I headed straight for the bathroom. I was alarmed because it felt like I had peed my pants on the walk home but, instead, I saw blood. I immediately thought I was in trouble, as if I had done something wrong. This rush of guilt consumed me. I was a bad girl. I was so scared and confused. As I sat there, thoughts raced through my head. *Am I going to die? How was I going to hide my underwear from anyone who might find them?* I eventually put on a new pair and hid the other in a garbage bag in the garage already full of trash.

At six years old, I was ashamed of what had happened, and I tried to hide the truth. I went to bed that night waking to nightmares of myself running through Ashley's court and through the other houses, frantically trying to get away from her uncle. It was the same dream that I would continue to have for years to come and one that would haunt me as an adult. The dream always ended the same. Once he reached out and grabbed me, I would wake in a cold sweat, terrified, eventually crying myself back to sleep.

It is never easy for me to revisit the traumatic events from my life, whether I am writing them down or standing on a stage speaking to three thousand people. However, I do it because, unlike my innocence, the one thing I have been able to reclaim is my voice. I speak for every abused child out there. It is therapeutic and empowering.

The physical pain from the rape was awful, but the emotional pain it would bring was far greater than I could have ever imagined. My innocence was stolen, my trust taken, and my voice silenced. As humans, we all have the ability to adapt to injury, whether physical or emotional. The little girl that I had been was forced to adapt to this horrific injury to such a young, little, innocent body and mind. My life from that day forward forever changed. Nobody knew what happened, nor could anyone have ever predicted that one day, the little girl I was would someday be described in headlines as "The Guardian Angel."

Chapter 1

Warning Signs

**THERE IS NO GREATER AGONY
THAN BEARING AN UNTOLD
STORY INSIDE YOU.**

—Maya Angelou

The psychological impact on a child who has been raped or molested is so damaging. While there was no hiding the sudden change in my behavior after being raped, nobody knew the important questions to ask to get the silent little girl that I was to speak out about the horror I had endured. Instead, I acted out.

In February 1992, just a few weeks after the rape, Grandpa was babysitting my older sister and me. My sister had upset me after taking off my shoes. As she dangled them in front of my face, taunting me, I screamed for her to give them back. Images flooded my mind all at once, hitting me like a ton of bricks. Suddenly, I saw Ashley's uncle on top of me struggling to get my shoes off as I fought so desperately to keep them on. I screamed at my sister even louder as the tears streamed down my face. It felt like I was being assaulted all over again.

I eventually made my way over to the door that led to my grandparent's backyard and began banging on it with both fists, crying uncontrollably. Suddenly, in just under a minute, my left hand went through the glass door. I stood there, shocked. I remember fear and panic coming over me, knowing I was going to be in trouble for breaking the glass.

Little had I realized, there was blood pouring down my arm from a large cut in my wrist. I escaped back into the kitchen in search of my grandpa, who had run down the hallway to retrieve my shoes from my sister. When he discovered what happened, I was rushed to the hospital where I had emergency surgery. Afterward, I woke up to find a pink cast on my arm.

Due to this and numerous other documented angry outbursts, my school decided to do a case study on me in April 1992, which resulted in my receiving an Individual Education Plan (IEP). In light of my social and emotional problems, I was labeled as having a behavior disorder. This was just three months after the rape.

Goals were set into place to help me develop appropriate ways of managing and resolving my anger and to develop a positive self-concept and self-image. In April 1992, my teacher noted on my report card: "Erin has had an extremely hard time with the injury to her arm and has acted in an extremely angry fashion when she has had to refrain from participating in recess or P.E. I am concerned about the way she handles frustrating situations and about the way she relates to her peers. We need to work together to learn to help Erin learn some constructive ways to deal with her anger and frustration."

All the warning signs were there twenty years ago, and the school made great efforts, pouring hundreds of hours into me with specialists working hard to help me to resolve my anger issues. However, the elements they missed in me then, and the elements they continue to miss in children today, are key to the changes I am trying to make in this world. The screaming tantrums I had in the hallways at school, with tears pouring down my face, and the crying on the floor of the school psychologist's office while pounding my fists into the ground are just a few.

A behavior specialist made me look at my arm when my cast came off and asked me to remember that whenever I felt like hurting myself to look at the scar on my wrist as a reminder not to. Little did she know, I was carrying an invisible scar.

By the time I reached second grade, my parents sat down with my sisters and me and told us we were moving. Not far, we would still be living in the same town, but it would require attending a new school in the same district. For a girl labeled with a behavior disorder with a lot of anger, a move could have possibly sent me over the edge. But instead, the transition went smoothly, which surprised many. On the very first day at my new school, I was able to make many new friends, friends who continue to be in my life to this day. Many stood alongside me at my wedding on August 10, 2013.

We moved in November 1993, and by April 1994, it was time for my annual IEP conference. For two years, I lived with the labels of "behavior disorder" and "emotionally disturbed child," but after five months at my new school, the education committee reported that I was no longer eligible for special education services and would be discontinued from the program. The progress report stated:

> Erin transferred from Campanelli in mid-November of 1993. She was receiving fifty minutes per week of Special Service Resource Program. She has made the transition to Blackwell very well, and her performance has been consistent. Minutes were decreased to thirty and Erin has continually been successful both behaviorally and academically. Erin has reached her goals in developing a positive self-concept/self-image. She thinks before she acts, which shows Erin independently problem-solving when she is in an angry situation.
>
> Positive reinforcement, weekly progress reports, sticker charts, and discussions regarding choices and responsibilities have all been utilized to help Erin maintain her success. It is recommended that Erin be terminated from the SSRP for the 1994–1995 school year. She will be in transition for two quarters to facilitate her transition to third grade.

The anger in me was gone, and it was like a complete transformation. I was a happy, outgoing kid who made new friends easily. My outbursts were brushed off as if I were just going through a phase and outgrew it once we moved—a mistake too many people make when a child's behavior changes.

This change in me was documented at the IEP conference that discontinued services for me. Conferences are held annually to review the progress of children in special education. My mother also noticed a change for the positive in me: "Erin's behavior is appropriate at home and has much improved." The speech pathologist reported that my speech and communication was an area of strength for me with age-appropriate skills, and that I had also shown significant improvement in memory.

The social worker I saw for thirty minutes a week as part of the behavior disorder resource reported that I had little outward conflict with others, that I voiced a desire to be cooperative toward teachers and peers, and that I limited myself to only expressing feelings in appropriate ways. He noted that I made a good adjustment to the new school, and he also reported that I was able to identify causes of behavior choices and was consistent about making better choices. He stated that I had found acceptable means of self-expression and that I was a very pleasant, charming student.

So just what had changed in me after moving to my new school over the five-month course from the angry eight-year-old that I was to the suddenly pleasant, charming student who was able to express herself appropriately? In 2011, I met with the behavior resource teacher who used to pull me out of class during my behavior disorder years. Over coffee, she confided in me that she and many other teachers were surprised to hear that I was doing so well at my new school and was being terminated from services. They even questioned whether or not they were talking about the same Erin whom they had known. One would think that relocating might upset a child with behavior issues; however, for me it was different. I carried with me the answers nobody else knew. Moving was my escape from repeated abuse. By alerting the world to this silent epidemic, I am hoping my efforts will prevent other children from ever having to endure such abuse.

I learned to adapt by keeping myself busy with my new friends in order to bury the pain I carried. I created new memories from lemonade stands, day camps and overnight camps, playing with dolls, building tree forts and snow forts, fishing, swimming, ice-skating, sledding, and so much more. While I appeared to heal on the outside, the past does not go away, and the psychological impact continued to affect my life.

When friends wanted me to have sleepovers, I was terrified. I feared their fathers or older brothers coming into the room at night and hurting me. I had every reason to think this way. I avoided sleepovers for the most part. I always wanted my friends to have the sleepover at my house. I used to have one of my friends lock her bedroom door when we went to bed at night. She never asked why, but I did it to protect myself from the men in her house.

Chapter 2

Slumber Party Danger

NOTHING MAKES US
SO LONELY AS OUR SECRETS.

—*Paul Tournier*

The sexual abuse began with Ashley's uncle Richard when I was six years old. It began with fondling, then progressed to oral sex, and eventually rape. The abuse continued for the next two and a half years until a month before my family and I moved. I was eight and a half years old when his physical terror over me ended.

I didn't have the language to express to anyone what was happening. Nobody had ever talked to me about sexual abuse. The only messages I was given were by the man raping me, and those were threats to keep me quiet. When he would tell me, "I know where you live. I will come get you if you tell anyone," this terrified me to my core. I remember lying in bed at night afraid that he was going to climb through my window, hide in my closet or under my bed, and wait for me. I began checking my closest methodically to make sure no one was there; otherwise, I could not fall asleep as a child. I remember at times jumping onto my bed—in the slightest chance he was under it—to prevent him from grabbing my legs and pulling me under. I had so much anxiety falling asleep.

Those thoughts kept me up at night or caused nightmares of him chasing me through different people's houses. I found myself screaming for someone to help me, but nobody came to my rescue. I recall the same reoccurring theme. Every house I ran through would be brightly lit with people inside but, no matter how loud I would scream, nobody seemed to notice.

The dream mirrored my reality. I acted out to get someone—anyone—to hear my pleas for help without actually saying what happened. Unfortunately, all the red flags I displayed were missed. Had someone talked to me at a young age about not keeping these types of secrets, I may have been saved from years of sexual abuse. Instead,

I listened to the only message I was getting from my abuser—to stay silent.

Just before I moved in the fall of 1993, Ashley and I found ourselves classmates again. We were now in the second grade and had rekindled our friendship. She had invited me to her ninth birthday party. I didn't want to go at first but, since I was moving the following month, I thought this might be the last time I saw my best friend. I also knew that there were going to be several other girls spending the night, too.

After a fun night of presents and cake, it was time to settle down and watch a movie. Just before the movie started, I got up to use the bathroom. As I closed the door to the bathroom, I noticed Ashley's uncle—who I had not seen all night—had his bedroom door cracked open. I felt a wave of fear spread over me. I thought, *Would he try to hurt me later that night?* After opening the door to leave the bathroom, I was abruptly pushed back in. I did not scream; I just stood in complete and utter fear, looking up at the man who had sexually assaulted me repeatedly before. It was like nearly every other time he ever abused me; I just froze in fear. He had his finger in front of his lip, tapping it to signal me to stay quiet. For one last time, he proceeded to assault me, going up my nightgown and having oral sex with me. I didn't scream for Ashley's mom. I was too scared. Instead, I stayed silent and took the abuse. Unlike being raped, where I did scream out, the oral sex never hurt. So it was easy for me to be quiet when it happened.

I was a little girl who had every right to be angry. Unfortunately, the school only went as far as to label me with an emotional and behavioral disorder. The school failed to educate and empower me to use my voice if I were ever sexually threatened or abused. They drilled tornado drills, fire drills, and bus drills into my head every year, yet I never had to take cover because of a tornado, run out of a burning building, or evacuate a school bus due to an emergency. In spite of all that, I knew exactly what to do in each of those incidents because we were educated. But what I really needed to know was how to escape a rapist; however, instead of being taught how to tell, I was being told that this was "our little secret" and that I would be hurt if I told anyone.

I continued to see the school social worker once a week at my new school even after other services were discontinued. When he pulled me out of class, we would talk and play games; however, I had an uneasy feeling around him. I hated giving him eye contact. Something about him didn't feel right, and my gut feeling at ten years old told me that something was off about this man. One day, he came to get me from class and we proceeded with our regular routine. I picked out a game as we talked about my academic challenges and family. I began talking about my older sister Caitlin, stating how she was now in junior high. The social worker asked me, "Does Caitlin wear a bra or a training bra?" The question sent a shock of emotions through me. I was confused and embarrassed as to why the social worker would ask me this. Quickly, I replied, "I don't know." I felt really uncomfortable and just wanted to go back to class.

I went home that day and told my mom immediately what the social worker at school asked me. My mother was stunned. She called the school and told the principal how out of line the social worker was for asking me that, and she told him that she wanted the social worker to have absolutely no contact with me ever again. I knew how strange it had been for the social worker to ask me that. The principal took my mother seriously and said he would speak with the social worker and make sure he no longer had any contact with me.

It was the topic around the dinner table that night, and we all agreed how creepy his question was. I found myself wishing that I had the same ability to tell my mother about the abuse I had endured as a young child the way I told her about the inappropriate question the school social worker had asked that day. As an adult, I would later find out that this social worker said very inappropriate comments to female faculty at the school as well.

I entered fifth grade in the fall of 1996. I had just finished fourth grade, which was my favorite year of school. I had an excellent teacher, amazing friends in class, and I loved what we had learned that year. I made so many fun memories, including a field trip to the state capital, where we sat as a class in the Senate chambers and listened in as legislators debated on laws. We also saw many historical sites, including President Abraham Lincoln's memorial. I was hoping fifth grade was going to be as fun as fourth. Little did I know how wrong I was.

Chapter 3

Familial Betrayal

I'M REALLY SCARED
AND CONFUSED; SOMETHING
HAPPENED LAST NIGHT
AND I DON'T KNOW
WHO TO TELL.

—*Erin Merryn, September 1996*

While spending the night at my grandparents' condominium in Lake Geneva, Wisconsin, in September 1996, I woke to find my older teen cousin Brian with his hand moving around in my vagina. I immediately grabbed his sweaty hand and pulled it from my pants. As I placed it back on his chest, I wondered just how long he had been molesting me. In that moment, there was a cold stare between the two of us, and then he shut his eyes. I blinked a few times, hoping that it was only a nightmare, but soon I realized that it wasn't. It proved to be another haunting image I would not be able to erase from my mind. He never said a word. I curled up in a ball facing away from him, wishing the sun would rise so I could get away from him.

The memories of being abused at six years old immediately resurfaced after waking to another man molesting me. I was disgusted and felt like I was going to throw up the pizza we had eaten that night for dinner. I was so confused. It was the start of a new, very painful chapter in my life, a chapter that I would once again be keeping silent about.

Who was Brian? Brian was more than just my cousin. He was someone I loved and trusted. He was that older brother I had never had, since I came from a family of girls. I looked up to him. We came from a close, tight-knit family that saw each other regularly, not just for the holidays. He lived with his family just down the street from mine. I never felt in danger from him.

I couldn't look at him the next morning. I tried to convince my eleven-year-old self it was all an awful dream. It really didn't happen. I knew that if I looked at him, it would only confirm what I so desperately wanted to believe was a nightmare. As I continued to avoid eye contact, I could feel his eyes on me all morning. Eventually, we locked eyes, and it was a cold, intimidating stare.

When I eventually made it home that night, I went straight up to my bedroom and opened my diary. It was where I had been writing about school, birthday parties, lemonade stands, the play I was in, and other life events. But suddenly, it turned into a place where I was writing about stolen innocence.

Over the course of the next six months, I saw my cousin Brian during the holidays, family gatherings, when my parents would decide to have dinner at his parents' house, or when he and his family would have dinner at ours. My cousin never tried to do anything to me during those six months, but I made sure to keep my distance from him.

I passed by my aunt and uncle's house every day on the way to school. By the spring of 1997, Brian's mother began asking me to watch my little cousins out of convenience while she ran errands. One was three and the other six. When she was gone, I would play Nintendo, take them to the park, and we would play hide-and-seek—their favorite pastime.

One day, my aunt had stopped me after school to ask me to babysit. I never hesitated to say yes since I always had fun with my little cousins. On this particular spring day, we were playing hide-and-seek when my cousin Brian came home. He asked what we were doing and proceeded to tell me that he had the perfect hiding place. As his six-year-old brother began counting, Brian led me down to the basement and toward a raised crawl space where Christmas items, other family belongings, and several sleeping bags and blankets were stored. Brian told me to climb up and lie down. He then covered me with an orange blanket. He said his brother would never find me there. I immediately became very nervous. Something didn't feel right. It was like I was sensing something terrible was about to happen.

Brian didn't leave as I had suspected he would. Instead, he lifted the blanket and got on top of me. Soon he had his hands down my pants rubbing my vagina. Then he began to dry hump me. I repeatedly told him to get off me and to stop. I tried pushing him off, but he was too strong for me.

Suddenly, the door opened, and Brian froze. So did I. We didn't utter a word as we heard his six-year-old brother walk in and a minute later walk out after failing to find us. Brian continued to abuse me until we heard his mother's high heels tapping across the laundry room floor directly above us. Brian whispered in my ear, "This is our secret. Don't tell anyone. They won't believe you."

I would hear those words repeatedly over the next year as Brian continued to sexually abuse me. He assaulted me whenever he had the opportunity. He forced himself on me several times in his bedroom. He assaulted me in his parent's walk-in closet, bathroom shower, and even in their bed. He molested me numerous times in his basement and in other random places, such as cars, the garage, his family room, and other relatives' homes during Thanksgiving and Christmas holidays, and during many other celebrations when we typically gathered as a large family.

It didn't matter if I was alone with his two little brothers babysitting or in a house with more than thirty relatives, he didn't care. He went after me whenever he had the opportunity, and he always found ways to trap me, silence me, and sexually abuse me. He chased me through relatives' homes and his own until he got me where he wanted me, ultimately feeding his sexual urge.

I kept it as a secret locked away in my diary, naively believing every word Brian told me—that no one would believe me, and that I had no proof if I told. It was a secret that would eventually rip my family apart.

Chapter
4

Finding My Vision

THE EYES ARE THE WINDOW TO YOUR SOUL.

—English Proverb

It was supposed to be a routine eye exam performed by the school nurse in April 1996, just five months before my cousin Brian's abuse began. I was in fourth grade, and the school was performing standard vision and hearing tests on all its students. I remember walking into the hallway, holding my little blue card, and waiting for my name to be called. I had worn glasses since the second grade for reading, but I rarely wore them. As I attempted to focus my eyes on the tiny letters to read back to the nurse, my stomach tightened. I could not see them. She made a note and informed my parents that I needed to be seen by an eye doctor for a follow-up. Little did I realize the complexities of failing an eye exam and what was to come.

The week after the exam, my dad took me to an eye doctor who performed another eye exam on me. I will never forget that day because of what happened next. After the doctor examined my eyes, he told me that he needed to talk to my dad alone. The observant eleven-year-old that I was knew something wasn't right, and I immediately became concerned as my dad went into the doctor's office, closing the door behind him. As I stood peering at all the eyeglasses lining the walls of the eye doctor's office, I began to pace nervously. Soon my dad returned with a look of worry on his face. I chose not to ask him what he had just discussed with the doctor. I figured that if there was something I needed to know, he would tell me. After all, these were my eyes we were talking about.

Both my parents sat me down the next night and said they needed to tell me something important. I knew it had to do with my eyes and patiently waited to hear what could have possibly been so bad to have my parents so seemingly on edge.

"Erin, the doctor found a problem in your eyes. The blood vessels are attacking the cornea, which is eating away at your vision. The blood vessels think there is an infection, but it is really taking your vision, and if we don't get you to see a specialist, you will go blind," my mother explained.

As I tried processing what I had just heard, I felt like my head was spinning. *Wait. Did they just say, "Go blind?"* I already felt as if I were in the dark most of the time, hiding the abuse in my life. The thought of actually going blind with darkness all around me petrified me.

By this time, I had already undergone one operation at five years old as a result of being born with underdeveloped tear ducts, which had caused my eyes to overproduce tears. People were always asking if I was crying. I came home from school often distraught, asking my mom, "When will people stop asking me if I am crying?" My mother would respond, "Tell them you are crying for all the poor kids in the world."

Doctors tried to fix the problem when I was five. While the tears were reduced, they still overproduced. I was teased often and called a crybaby by some kids. I learned to eventually ignore the bullies and pretend I didn't hear them. I noticed that if I didn't give them any type of reaction, they would get bored and move on. The same was true when two boys asked why I was older than our other classmates were. Before I could answer, they said, "You flunked. You're stupid." It hurt inside, but I pretended their comments didn't faze me.

As I entered fifth grade, I was already seeing two specialists. My underdeveloped tear ducts had nothing to do with this medical condition, and one of my specialists explained to me that what I had was extremely rare in children. It was a condition often seen only in senior citizens. Despite my age, I spoke my mind as a child and instructed my doctors not to keep anything from me. There would be no talking to my parents in private. "These are my eyes," I told them. "You tell me what is happening, and what we will do next." I was a little pistol.

Dr. Mack was very concerned and very forward about what would happen. He explained to me that I would eventually need surgery and that if we did not stay on top of this, I would eventually go blind in both eyes. A part of me didn't want to take him seriously. It was terrifying to think about for anyone at any age, but especially so for a child.

Throughout the course of fifth grade, I gradually lost vision in my right eye completely. I would close my left and everything would blur. I couldn't see anything out of it. My left eye, which I called my good eye as a kid, continued to have perfect 20/20 vision whenever I read the charts. I had my first operation a week after sixth grade ended, and I underwent three more operations throughout my seventh-grade year.

The first operation consisted of cutting open my left eyelid and tightening the muscle. My right eyelid was lazy. It always lay on the cornea, causing oil to build up on the eye, which was partly to blame for my vision being destroyed. My doctor had to guess about how much to tighten the muscle. Since I was under anesthesia, there was no way of knowing if he was tightening it too much. If he did, my eyelid wouldn't close completely, so he had to be very careful. Ultimately, he ended up not tightening it enough.

The next surgery involved placing tubes into my tear ducts. That surgery hurt a lot. I came home and blood just kept pouring from my nose. I was in so much pain. I hated those tubes. You could see them and eye boogers always built up around them. It was nasty. I was thrilled when, after just a few short months, I went back under anesthesia to have the tubes removed.

I was always scared before surgery because I feared being put to sleep. Due to the abuse I had previously endured, I was afraid that things would be done to me while I was unconscious. This was logical since the abuse occurred while I was sleeping. After my last operation, I woke up in recovery punching, kicking, and screaming. It took six nurses and two doctors to hold me down. I have no memory of it, but I was told how the scene unfolded by my doctor when he came to check on me in the recovery room.

The final operation—the only one I was not put to sleep for—was laser eye surgery. Dr. Mack knew that to restore my vision, I needed the laser surgery; however, he was extremely concerned about doing such a procedure on someone as young as I was. The surgery is such a delicate process that the slightest movement could cause permanent damage to the eye. Dr. Mack had to put total faith and trust in me to lie completely still. I was told my mother would be allowed in the operating room to hold my hand.

Dr. Mack led the two of us down the hall to the operating room where his assistants were waiting. I positioned myself onto a reclining chair, and a warm blanket was placed over me. I soon found myself gazing up at the medical equipment above me. I had so much anxiety, and, while confident in my doctor's abilities, I was still terrified he would make a mistake.

My doctor appeared wearing special surgical glasses. He placed a medical tool around my right eye to prevent me from closing it. From there, he prepped the eye with numbing drops. Shortly after, he held a sharp object that a nurse had handed to him and began scrapping away at my cornea. In the room, my eye was displayed on a huge screen that my mother and doctor were able to view. My mother couldn't believe what she was seeing. It must have been a frightful sight for her, watching the doctor take what looked like a knife to my eye. I didn't budge the entire time. I was completely still. So still, you might have thought that they had put me to sleep.

When the surgery was over, they lifted me up and began calling my name. I wasn't responding. Just then, the spunky girl that I was cracked a huge smile, throwing them all into a bout of laughter.

Afterward, Dr. Mack told me that I had done better than any adult he had ever worked on. He was taken aback by how well the procedure went. Still, he warned my mom and me to expect extreme pain once the numbness wore off and advised us to pick up the medication I needed at the pharmacy immediately to manage the pain. He said that the pain usually set in shortly after the medicine wore off, and that the day after is the worst part of the recovery process.

After surgery, I felt no pain. The next day I felt no pain. Days turned into weeks and I failed to experience any of the pain he had described. My doctor loved hearing this news, and each time he called in the hours and days after surgery, he would ask how the pain was. My parents would say, "She is in no pain at all."

Over the course of the next several months, I gradually began to see out of my right eye again. From fourth grade to seventh, my left eye's vision only changed from 20/20 to 30/20. My vision seemed to improve with each new day. My right eye, in which I was previously completely blind, eventually gained near perfect vision. With this finally behind me I started to look ahead to my future instead of dreading another operation. Despite this great news, my doctor warned me that the blood vessels he lasered away would eventually grow back, and when I reached my thirties or forties, I would need surgery again to prevent vision loss. I was glad to close this chapter of my life for a time and let go of the fear and anxiety from going blind and all the operations I endured. By this time I had overcome so much and was ready to move forward.

Today, I still have perfect vision in my left eye and my right eye is still right where it was after my last operation. I recently went back to see my eye doctor who had worked with me for approximately three years. He didn't recognize me. I was no longer the nervous kid with so many questions. When I told him who I was, he was excited to see me. He proceeded to examine my eyes, informing me that the blood vessels he lasered off were indeed growing back—as he had predicted—and that he would eventually have to raise the eyelid again and do another laser surgery. Since I still have my vision, I decided to do nothing and cross that bridge when I get there. The difference this time around is that I am no longer an abused little girl. Instead, I am a woman who has found her vision in life.

Chapter 5

Behind Closed Doors

BE STRONG AND COURAGEOUS.
DO NOT BE AFRAID OR TERRIFIED
BECAUSE OF THEM, FOR THE
LORD YOUR GOD GOES WITH YOU;
HE WILL NEVER LEAVE YOU
NOR FORSAKE YOU.

—*Deuteronomy 31:6*

One Friday afternoon in the winter of 1998, my aunt called me panicked. Her other babysitter had just canceled. She needed me to watch my cousins because she and my uncle had an event in Chicago to attend. I suggested that she ask one of her other boys, either Brian or his brother Mike. She told me that both of them had hockey games and were spending the night with friends. Because Brian was going to be gone and I could hear the desperation in my aunt's voice, I agreed.

The night went smoothly. I made the young boys macaroni and cheese, played Nintendo with them, and read them stories before bed. I then went into Aunt Mary and Uncle Scott's bedroom to watch television because she told me I could stay in there in case four-year-old Jake woke up. While watching TV, I heard noises coming from downstairs, but I figured it was my imagination and that I was getting myself freaked out over nothing. It sounded as if someone was walking around. I kept looking at the bedroom door, which I had left slightly ajar, convinced that someone was going to appear. After hearing the sounds three or four times, I told myself that it was just the furnace and proceeded to turn up the television to drown out the noise.

Moments later, I heard the noise yet again, but much closer this time. I shot a look at the bedroom door again, this time jumping as panic came over me. Brian stood there with a stone-cold face, staring me down. I jumped off the bed, scrambling for words. "Why are you home?" I demanded. As I looked across the room at my cousin, a sick grin stretched across his face. I knew I was in trouble the second I saw him.

"My game was canceled, and I decided to come home instead of staying the night at my friend's like I had planned," he said. I knew he could see the fear in my eyes and hear it from the quivering in my voice.

"This mom on television is dying, and she is making home videos for her little daughter to watch through different events in her life," I told him, trying anything to distract him from the sick thoughts I knew were going through his head.

He closed the distance between us. My only chance of saving myself was to get out of the bedroom. As I climbed across the bed, Brian shot around it and jumped for my ankle. Grabbing it, he flipped me over. I fought with him as he sat on top of me, holding down my hands in an attempt to restrain me. His disgusting grin angered me. How could he find so much pleasure in terrifying me? I feared looking into his eyes. When I did, all I saw was evil. I wanted to spit in his face as he laughed at my struggles to fend him off.

With one hand still free, I did what I had never done before. I punched Brian in the balls. He fell off me, and I pulled myself together and ran for the door. I did not look back. I ran downstairs and didn't stop until I reached the family room. Standing stock-still, I looked out the window toward my house, contemplating running the whole way home. But I feared he would just chase after me, drag me into the marsh's tall grass, and rape me right there. I prayed that he would leave me alone and stay upstairs, but, five short minutes later, I heard the sound of his footsteps coming down the stairs. It was the same noise that I had thought was just the furnace moments earlier.

I wanted someone to save me. I wanted to curl up into a ball and cry because I knew he was coming for me. I moved into the kitchen and waited for him. With my heart racing at what seemed like a hundred miles per hour, my eyes darted between both kitchen entrances. I did not know which one Brian would appear from. The instant he came around the corner, I ran. I ran in circles from the kitchen to the dining room through the living room and then the foyer. It was like being in a horror movie, but this was real. I was living it, and I did not know how to make it stop or how it was going to end.

He stopped chasing me without warning, and the house grew silent. I knew he was hiding somewhere in the living room. It then occurred to me that I had only one choice before he was able to trap me: run upstairs, wake my little cousins, and hold them. I rationalized that this would keep him off me.

Without thinking for another moment, I shot upstairs. Brian popped out around the corner and chased after me. By the time I reached the boys' door, Brian caught up to me and forced me to close the door just as I peered in to see my two little cousins sound asleep.

In that moment, I just wanted to disappear. He pulled me back into his parents' room and onto their bed. I begged him not to have sex with me. Before I knew it, he was back on top of me. I tried pushing him off, but he would only grab my wrists, hold them above my head, and laugh. I felt his pounding heart against my chest. His breathing was heavy and hot against my ear. As he pulled his hands through my hair, the hairs on my arms stood straight. Then I felt Brian unzipping my pants. Tears welled up in my eyes. I was so scared of what he was going to do next.

I glanced at the clock. To this day, the red numbers 9:38 are burned into my memory. Every minute felt like an hour. My aunt and uncle were not going to be home until around 1:00 AM. As he yanked my jeans down around my thighs and began forcing his fingers up inside me, I realized that if I was going to make it through the night, I had to focus on something to distract me from the pain he was putting me through. I didn't have the strength left to force him off me. I was exhausted and every time I tried he would pinch me really hard. I gave up the fight and just lay there. I lay motionless with my eyes closed. I kept telling myself that he would do his business and then leave me alone, but I realized that with each minute that passed, he wasn't leaving. At one point, he had one of his hands on my vagina and the other hand raking his fingers through my hair as he whispered dirty things in my ear. I lay there staring at the ceiling wondering when this hell I was in would be over.

After moving up and down on me for some time, he stopped and grabbed my hand. I tried to pull away, but he was too strong. He placed my hand on his penis. I kept saying "No" or "Stop it!" But he refused, forcing my fist open and making me wrap my hand around his penis. Then he wrapped his hand around mine and began moving it up and down. The longer it went on the more aggressive he became, and I began to fear the worst; that he was going to rape me. "Please don't have sex with me," I begged once again.

"I know where condoms are," he said.

"No! No! No! Please don't do it." Tears were streaming down my face. I had already experienced the worst pain of my life when I was raped as a little girl. I never wanted to experience that pain again and was terrified I was about to.

Suddenly, his face was between my legs and he was sucking on me and sticking his tongue inside my vagina. I was so disgusted, but it didn't hurt, so I didn't fight him. I knew the pain I would experience if he had intercourse with me. I was praying he would not go beyond having oral sex with me.

I closed my eyes—the television still played in the background—trying to imagine myself somewhere warm, but, when that did not work, I focused on the sounds of the passing cars on the street, praying that one would be my aunt and uncle coming home. The abuse went on for two hours, two of the worst hours of my life.

At 12:05, I heard another car coming down the street, but this one seemed to slow down. I had never been so happy to hear the sound of a garage door opening. I had prayed for God to bring my aunt and uncle home early, and here they were pulling into the garage an hour sooner than expected. Relief swept over me. Brian's face lifted from my crotch and his evil grin was replaced with a look of sheer panic. I'm convinced that if they had come home an hour later like they had planned, he would have had intercourse with me that night. But God answered my prayers and brought them home early.

At the sound of his parents returning, Brian jumped off me like lightning. He adjusted himself and made his way to the door. Then he stopped, turning to face me. "This is our secret. It never happened," he said. And with that, he disappeared.

Chapter 6

Breaking the Silence

THEY STOLE MY INNOCENCE,
TOOK MY TRUST, BUT I RECLAIMED
MY VOICE, AND THAT VOICE WILL
NEVER BE SILENCED AGAIN.

—*Erin Merryn*

I t was a beautiful, sunny day in April 1998, as my mother, eleven-year-old sister, and I made our way from the parking lot up to the door of a building built in 1895 that used to be an old white farmhouse. I walked in, pondering whether or not these people were against me or if they were questioning if my sister and I were telling the truth. I was terrified.

As we opened the door, bells rang, notifying others that we were coming in. A woman who introduced herself as Larissa greeted us. She had us sit in a waiting room filled with toys, games, videos, and a television. My mother went into an office with Larissa, who told us that she just had some paperwork she needed to fill out with Mom.

My sister and I sat there waiting nervously. We could hear our mother crying, even though the door to the office was closed.

"I failed my kids. How did I not know?" she cried.

Twenty minutes passed before the door opened again. By then, my sister and I were watching a movie. When she came out, my mother's eyes were bloodshot. Larissa asked my sister and me if we wanted something to eat. We nodded, and she gathered up some bagels and orange juice for us.

Suddenly, a woman appeared from around the corner. As she approached, she introduced herself as Meghan. She told me that I would be going into an office to speak with her, and then my sister Allie would meet with her after me. She pointed to some stuffed animals on the floor by the secretary's desk and told us that when we were done, we could pick out and keep any stuffed animal we wanted. This excited me because I had always loved stuffed animals. We received one for Christmas every year.

"Erin, we are going to start with you since you're the older sister. Can you follow me?" she asked.

I followed Meghan down a hallway lined with stuffed animals. When we reached the back, there were two rooms, and she asked me which one I would prefer talking to her in. I picked the very colorful room filled with stuffed animals, beanbags, and a blue table with chairs.

"Where do you want to sit, at the table or on a beanbag chair?" she casually asked. What she hadn't known was that during one of the times I had been sexually abused by my cousin, I was held down on a beanbag chair.

"I will sit at the table," I said.

As I sat down nervously, I noticed a large mirror inset into the wall, which felt oddly out of place. *Why?* I wondered. Such a huge mirror for a small room.

This stranger began asking me questions about school, my friends, and my plans for the summer. She was trying to get to know who I was. After receiving answers to many of her questions, she looked at me and asked, "Do you know the difference between the truth and a lie, and will you be willing to tell the truth today?"

I already feared they wouldn't believe me, just like my cousin had said, and now I was being asked if I was going to tell the truth. After agreeing to tell the truth, I looked at her and said, "That is why I did not tell before."

Meghan prodded me for clarification.

"I didn't say anything because I was afraid no one would believe me. Sometimes I play jokes on people, so if I told what Brian had done, they would think I was just making another joke."

In that moment, I felt ashamed and dirty. Thoughts of abuse ran through my head. A part of me was afraid to share with her what I had gone through because I feared she would judge me for not telling when Brian abused me the first time. I felt like it was my fault that my sister had been abused, too.

"If I had just told when it first happened, my sister would have never been abused," I proclaimed.

Two weeks after the last time Brian assaulted me, my younger sister Allie told me Brian had been sexually abusing her. She had no idea he was doing the same thing to me. Being her older sister, it devastated me, and guilt immediately consumed me. It was then that I realized that if I had spoken up when the abuse first began, she would never have been hurt by him.

I was fighting back the tears as Meghan reached across the table. Holding my hand, she said, "It isn't your fault. You did absolutely nothing wrong. Everything is going to be alright. Erin, you are safe now. Nobody is going to hurt you anymore."

Meghan then asked if I would talk to her about what my cousin Brian would do. Her comforting words had given me the confidence to share with her what happened behind closed doors—the things I was told to never tell anyone.

I stared at the large mirror on the wall and began sharing details with her about what had happened. It was the first time light was being shone on the darkness I carried. I was breaking my silence. My voice was finally being heard, and I was telling it to a complete stranger.

I began sharing the details starting from the beginning of that very first night I woke up to him molesting me to the weeks, months, and nearly two years of abuse that followed.

At one point in the interview, Meghan stopped me and from underneath the table she pulled out two anatomical dolls. Anatomical dolls are special dolls used specifically for investigating sexual abuse cases.

Meghan asked me if I could show her, with the dolls, what Brian did to me. I was hesitant at first, but I picked up the two dolls and began showing her the ways in which Brian had sexually abused me. As I put the dolls on top of each other, I suddenly saw his face flash before me. It was like I was reliving the abuse all over again.

Meghan saw the distress I was in and said, "Let's take a break, and we'll continue in a little bit."

After a short break, I went back into the room and continued to share with her what Brian had done to me. She told me how brave I was for telling. She told me that I would start to feel better after telling someone what happened instead of holding it in. She was right. I was already beginning to feel the relief from talking about what had been bottled up inside me for so long. I couldn't tell her everything. It was too uncomfortable for me to talk about all that he had done to me, especially that last night.

I was never asked if anyone else had ever hurt me the way Brian did. I think if I was asked, I might have shared what happened when I was six, seven, and eight. Instead, I protected my already devastated parents from knowing that secret by withholding those details from her. I didn't want to upset my parents any more than they already were. My dad was staying strong for Mom, who never seemed to stop crying since she had learned the news a month earlier.

"Did you ever tell anyone what your cousin did to you?" Meghan asked.

"Yes, my best friend Emily. I told her six months ago at a sleepover and made her promise she would not tell anyone."

As we finished, Meghan leaned down and met my eyes. "You did a wonderful job, Erin. Before I send you back to your mom in the waiting room, can you tell me what you would like to see happen to your cousin?"

"I think he should do counseling and community service," I said. Even after all he had put me through, I didn't want to see him go to jail.

As I left the room, I took something with me that I had lost a long time ago. I had reclaimed my voice. I was no longer living in silence about my cousin. While he had finished killing off what innocence I had left from being raped when I was younger, and destroyed my ability to trust, I wasn't going to give him control over my voice anymore.

When I walked back into the waiting room, my sister was there watching a movie and coloring. I could tell how nervous she was. "You have nothing to worry about," I told her in an attempt to calm her nerves. "The woman is a really nice person."

"How did it go? I am really proud of you, Erin. I'm so sorry you had to go through this," my mother said as she hugged me.

When my aunt and uncle decided not to cooperate with my parents by getting Brian the psychological help he needed, my parents got the authorities involved. They soon learned that Brian had repeatedly denied what had happened to his parents. A detective assigned to our case referred our family to the Children's Advocacy Center of Northwest Cook County, Illinois. I never imagined that this place, a place I had never heard of before until now, would eventually hold so much meaning and appreciation in my heart.

When my sister returned to the waiting room, our mother was led upstairs to talk with the advocate, therapist, and police detective who had been behind the inset two-way mirror on the wall watching our entire interview, a fact that I didn't learn until three weeks after our interview.

My sister and I talked about our interviews after the adults disappeared. "What room did you pick?" my sister asked.

"The colorful room," I replied.

"Me, too," she said. "I sat on the beanbags. I didn't like using the dolls to show what he did to me."

"I was really uncomfortable with that, too," I explained.

You have to understand something about my sister and me. We loved playing dolls along with our best friend Emily. We played house all the time. We all got very expensive baby dolls the year before. We would push our strollers to the local park often. We would take our babies on picnics with us, to sleepovers, and we even threw birthday parties for our baby dolls. I always said as a kid, "I don't care what people think of me. I am never going to stop playing with dolls, even when I am in high school." We never thought we would have to use dolls to act out the sexual abuse our cousin did to us. After that, I never looked at dolls the same way again and stopped playing with them immediately.

My sister and I distracted ourselves with a board game while the movie *Charlie and the Chocolate Factory* played in the background. In another room, my mom was being briefed on what would happen next, which involved bringing our cousin Brian into the police station for questioning.

Just as Allie and I began to ponder over which stuffed animals we wanted to take home, our mom, an advocate, and a forensic interviewer appeared. Larissa and Meghan proceeded to tell us how proud they were of us.

"For being so brave today, go pick out any stuffed animal you want," Larissa said.

I immediately went to a teddy bear that had caught my attention the minute we walked in.

As we made our way out of the Children's Advocacy Center that morning, I stood for a moment with the sun hitting my face and took in a deep breath of fresh air. The dark world I had been living in alone was suddenly not so dark and lonely anymore. I was so relieved someone else now knew, and that I would never be locked in a room with my cousin again. Healing could begin. I reclaimed my voice that day. Little by little, my voice, once silenced, would grow stronger and louder. Once just a girl lost in a world of terror and evil, I would soon find my way out and discover an incredible journey of grace, forgiveness, and freedom.

My cousin Brian confessed while being interviewed in police custody. My parents had the choice to take the case to trial, where my cousin would face jail time, or not take it to trial, at which time he would be screened through the court system, placed on probation, and receive psychological help. If they chose to take the case to trial, my sister and I would have to testify against our cousin. My parents did not want to put us through that. More than anything, we all really wanted him to get the help he needed.

Brian was given seven years of probation, 1,000 hours of community service, counseling, and he could not come within a hundred feet of my sister and me. We later learned that my aunt fought to get Brian's probation reduced to six months. She was able to get him out of a court-ordered treatment program and instead placed in private therapy of her choosing. The therapist later wrote a letter to the Illinois State's Attorney confirming that she had met with Brian a few times and that he admitted his wrongs and would not repeat them again. As a family, we were disappointed Brian never got the help we all knew he needed, and we feared what he might do to others.

Our relatives, who supported our cousin even after he confessed, ostracized us. It was too difficult for them to believe that a family member could do something so heinous. It was easier for them to be in denial about it, to sweep it under the rug, and pretend it never happened. Some thought my sister and I were lying and some brushed it off because he was just a teenager. Two family members even called the police department early on trying to get them to drop the charges against Brian. One sent a hate letter to my mother, and another said my sister and I voluntarily engaged in sex acts with our cousin. I am amazed by the lengths to which my extended family went to protect my cousin. It was extremely painful. I used to say often, "They weren't there. They have no idea the hell he put us through."

For the many years that followed, I was very angry over how they could stand by him and act as if nothing had happened. I have cried about it so much that I cannot cry about it anymore. I finally learned to accept them for who they are and that everyone is entitled to their own opinion. We all handle things differently. I would later come to discover as an adult that I should not judge them. God tells us to love our enemies, so that is what I have chosen to do. Incest destroys families. While the damage is done, there is still hope to repair some of those relationships. There was a period of time—approximately six years to be exact—when my family and I cut off all ties with most of my dad's family. We would cross paths in the grocery store with loved ones, whom we had once sat across from at Thanksgiving dinner, as if we were complete strangers. Today, much of that has changed. We are on much better terms with most. Much of that has to do with the grace and forgiveness we have shown to them.

Chapter 7

Academic Struggles

I'VE LEARNED THAT YOU
SHOULDN'T COMPARE YOURSELF
TO THE BEST OTHERS CAN DO, BUT
TO THE BEST YOU CAN DO.

—*Omer B. Washington*

lways feeling like a failure, I often called myself stupid as a child. No matter how hard I tried, I felt it didn't show. While I always did my homework in school and did well on it, along with the class projects, my mind would go blank when it came time to take my exams. I could not retain all the details I had studied the night before. I found it equally frustrating for most of my subjects, but math proved most challenging. When I would go to take an exam, I could only remember how to solve part of the math equation, which would result in me failing the test. I tried every suggestion that my teachers provided. I used flashcards, and I even met with the students I called the "smart kids," who would do study groups with me in elementary school.

Unlike many of my peers, who would be grounded for getting a "C" on a report card or failing an exam, I was fortunate to have parents who were easy on me. If my parents had raised me any other way, I would have been grounded until I graduated high school. While I failed exams often, my parents were able to see what my teachers could not. They saw me at home doing my homework and studying for exams.

At a parent-teacher conference the first semester of sixth grade, my teacher suggested to my parents that I get a private tutor to come once a week to help raise my math grade from a D. When my older sister Caitlin learned they were suggesting a tutor for me, she told my parents, "I'll tutor Erin, and you can pay me instead." That didn't last long. She spent one afternoon with me after school. She had little patience when it came to trying to teach me something that came so easy for her to understand yet was so difficult for me. Frustrated in her failed attempt at getting me to understand the concepts, she finally caved and told my mom that she could not tutor me.

After seeking out a few suggestions, we found a math tutor to come every Tuesday after school to help me for an hour with math. We did homework together, practiced problems, and prepared for exams. She always seemed to have so much confidence in me the week of an exam. But when it came time to take the test, I could only remember the first two steps to each equation, and then I was left guessing at what to do next. My exams were often returned with failing marks.

Being sexually abused definitely impacted my performance in school. I must emphasize that this is a warning sign in and of itself. If a child's grades drastically change, then something is not right. There were many times after being sexually abused by my cousin that I would find myself distraught the next day at school. During recess, while all my classmates would play, I can remember sitting with my back against the brick wall of the school, wanting nothing more than to be left alone. I would purposely isolate myself from others, which is yet another warning sign to be on the lookout for. The other kids who were there with me were those who had lost recess privileges due to behavior issues in class or from not doing their homework. It was a form of punishment, and here I was putting myself in my own time-out. These memories will never leave me nor will those feelings of isolation, sitting there alone against the wall of the school with clear blue skies on a bright, sunny day, watching my classmates scream, laugh, and run while I was replaying images of the horror I had endured the day before—horror that I was too afraid to share with anyone else.

My academic struggles continued in junior high and high school. Some of the comments on my report cards from my teachers said that I had difficulty applying prior learning, and test and quiz scores were low, but I was also a pleasure to have in class, my work showed improvement, and I had good class participation. It was so frustrating to be putting forth so much effort but not seeing results. I often found myself in tears over this.

What my teachers and parents were unaware of was what really impacted my academic performance. They recognized I was depressed, but they had no idea about the flashbacks and nightmares of my abuse—flashbacks that I could never have prepared myself for. One moment I could be fine, sitting in the school cafeteria eating lunch, and then suddenly I would be back in a bedroom being attacked by my cousin.

One day in seventh grade, I was walking to my class when I ran into my childhood friend Ashley. I had not seen her since we were young, when the abuse from her uncle had occurred. A flood of emotions hit me. Seeing her reminded me of her uncle and all that he had done to me: him coming into the bedroom molesting me, having oral sex with me, and raping me. This was something I had wanted to bury forever. We spoke for a few minutes and then went on to class. I was distraught the rest of the period as my mind was flooded with flashbacks.

That night, I was plagued by a recurring nightmare I had frequently had as a child, the one where her uncle chased me through the court where she lived while I screamed for a neighbor to help me. All the houses had their lights on as if the owners were home, but nobody ever came to my rescue. The nightmare always ended with me being assaulted by her uncle. In analyzing this nightmare today, I feel that the lights and my unanswered screams symbolized all the warning signs I displayed as a child, such as my behavior problems and the tantrums. Just like in my dreams, nobody ever came to rescue me from the horror I was living in.

By eighth grade, someone did recognize my struggles. I had an excellent math teacher named Mrs. Verstat who saw the effort I applied. Her comments on my report cards were always positive, stating that I consistently tried to do well. Mrs. Verstat recognized something else. One day after getting class started, she pulled me out into the hallway. We sat at a table and she proceeded to ask me why I had looked so unhappy over the course of the past several weeks. I explained to her how well my sisters did in school and how much I struggled, and that it wasn't fair. "Why can't I be like my sisters, both making honor roll or be like my older sister where it said on her report card last year she was number one of six hundred and sixty-four students? My parents are so proud of her. I have nothing to be proud of," I emphatically stated.

"Erin, you need to stop comparing yourself to your sisters and classmates. All that matters in the end is that you know you put forth the effort. You can still be just as successful in life as your sisters. Stop being so hard on yourself. I see that you try to do your best, and I know with determination you will be successful in life." I watched tears fill my teacher's eyes and recognized how much faith she had in me and the lesson she was trying to convey, for me to stop comparing myself to my sisters. "What matters is that I see that you are trying." Her words would echo back at me in the years to come.

Other teachers began to recognize my efforts, too, and they saw how depressed I had become. They knew something wasn't right. At a parent-teacher conference, they finally addressed their concerns to my parents. They explained to them that I had test anxiety. I knew this from an early age. The anxiety came from knowing just how much I had prepared for each exam, combined with the constant fear that I was going to fail. In the conference notes, they expressed a big change in my mood. I was not happy and had low test scores. In light of these findings, my mother decided to bring them up to speed on the abuse I had experienced and how it might be impacting me in school. It had been a year and a half since I had disclosed what had happened to me to the team at the Children's Advocacy Center, and, while the abuse may have ended, the flashbacks followed me.

My teachers decided to try something. A special education aide frequently came to help students with learning disabilities in a few of my classes. She would take the students into the hall during exams and read each exam question to them to help slow them down and force them to take their time instead of rushing through it. They hoped that by having someone read my exam to me outside the classroom, my test anxiety would be reduced.

When I first heard about the option of having my social studies and science exams read to me, I didn't like it. Students would notice I was leaving class and ask where I was going. I was encouraged not to let what others thought bother me, as it was none of their business. Yet, I was at that difficult stage in life where, in junior high, peers' judgments always seemed to matter. Regardless, I was told that having someone read my exams to me might help, so I decided to go with my teachers' suggestions. My teachers saw a major improvement in my exam grades. In social studies I got a B+ and an A- on my next two tests.

Just weeks before graduating from middle school, my physical education teacher pulled me aside during class while my other classmates were distracted playing a game. I had just failed my final exam, so he sat down with me on the gym floor and began reading every question on the test and asking me to give him the correct multiple choice answer. After going through the entire exam, he looked at me and said, "Erin, you answered every single one of those correctly, yet you failed it reading it to yourself. You need to make sure you let someone know when you get to high school about this so they can help you out." I always knew something wasn't right, since I wasn't lazy and I studied, but I just figured it was who I was and there was nothing that could be done to change it.

While I knew the flashbacks were impacting my academics, there was a part of me that knew that the abuse I had experienced did not hold all the blame. I was very self-aware and observant, and I knew something wasn't right in my brain. It would take years before I would learn just how right I was. At the time, I was so convinced that I even wrote about it in my fifth-grade journal. Here is an excerpt:

April 20, 1997

I feel a deep pain inside of me. There is so much going on in my life. My grades are bad; no matter how much effort I put into studying, it doesn't show. I study using flashcards and think I have the material down and end up failing the exam. I feel like there is something wrong inside my brain. It is like something is not connecting. So many things do not add up. I put forth effort in school and still struggle. I am going blind and being told I will need a bunch of operations to save my vision. I was born unable to smell anything. I do not know anyone that cannot smell. It all makes me wonder what is really going on in that brain of mine. Something is not right up there; I just don't know what it is, but I know it is something. It just seems everything I have trouble with is connected to my brain. I guess I will just always wonder and keep trying my best. At times it can just be so frustrating and scary when things are going on that you have no control over.

Chapter 8

Painful Memories

WHAT LIES BEHIND US
AND WHAT LIES BEFORE US ARE
TINY MATTERS COMPARED TO
WHAT LIES WITHIN US.

—*Ralph Waldo Emerson*

Others have always told me that junior high is the most difficult and challenging time in a youth's life. So as I walked up the steps of my high school for the very first time, I thought this was going to be an exciting new chapter for me. Little did I know it was going to challenge and teach me more than I could have ever imagined.

Looking back, I wish I could have had the wisdom I have now when I was in high school. Even though I had many strengths—which I failed to recognize until later in life—I would have chosen to take a completely different path and carried with me a completely different attitude. Just like any high school student, I had some maturing to do. I also had personal healing I needed to address.

It didn't take long for my academic struggles to show or for me to receive my first F on an exam. Algebra proved to be the most difficult. And the fact that I ended my day with it didn't help. I carried a negative attitude with me whenever I would walk into an exam room, undoubtedly affecting my performance.

"I studied last night, but guess what . . . I am still going to fail," I stated as I walked into math class on one particular afternoon.

My math teacher, Mr. Zickert, looked at me and said, "With that bad attitude, you will fail. You are setting yourself up for failure by saying that."

He marked on my midterm report card that I displayed a negative attitude. While I did not get it then, I would later come to understand his point and the importance of having a positive attitude to be successful in life. Even when things do not seem to be going your way, you cannot give up. This notion was the best thing he taught me that year, above and beyond any algebra equation. It was hard to implement though, as I became extremely frustrated when I attended class, did the work, studied, and still failed the exams. I should have been used to it by then, since this was how it was throughout elementary and middle school.

I didn't struggle academically at everything. It was mainly just the tests and quizzes that stumped me. Standing up in front of my peers or adults never scared me. I never got nervous like so many other people do. Public speaking is one of the leading fears people have, and yet it came natural to me. Tests may have given me anxiety, but public speaking certainly did not. When asked to speak in front of the class, I always felt confident.

In freshman English class, we had to give a timed, persuasive speech on a book. I chose to read *Alive*, the novel based on the 1972 airplane crash in the Andes Mountains. We were asked to draw a number so that we could determine the order in which everyone would present. I told my teacher Mr. Barons I would go first. One could always sense the fear and anxiety that filled the air as my classmates struggled to get the nerve to stand and give their speeches, but not me. It came naturally, and I got a kick out of taking the pressure off others just by volunteering. I stood up in front of my class, confident, smiling, and relaxed, and waited for my teacher to give me the cue to begin. I wasn't nervous at all as I started my speech with my classmates' full attention.

After relaying my final thoughts, Mr. Barons, who had been sitting in the back of the class grading me, jumped out of his seat with excitement, scaring half the class. "Ms. Merryn, in my thirty years of teaching, that was one of the best speeches I have ever heard from a student. You gave an exceptional speech and nailed every point. You were articulate, with a strong, clear voice, confident, had excellent content, great enthusiasm, engaging to the audience, perfectly paced, awesome eye contact, and had everyone's attention!" he exclaimed.

I was startled and did not know how to respond to his extremely positive response to my speech. All my peers stared at me in silence, and I suddenly realized the bar I had just set. I felt terrible for the person who had to go after me.

Mr. Barons talked about me in all his English classes that day, referring to my speech and how I delivered it. He was using me as an example of what to do if you wanted an A. My name was announced over the school's PA system the following Monday during morning announcements as a Saxon Pride Award Student. The Saxon Pride Award was a card that gave the recipient access into all the school sporting and dance events free, except for prom, along with many other perks. It was given in recognition for something excellent that a teacher saw in a student. Teachers were only allowed to give this award twice a year. The following letter was sent home to my parents.

March 12, 2001

Dear Mr. and Mrs. Merryn:

Congratulations on having a Saxon Pride Award winner. Erin's name was read Monday morning over the school's public address system. Award winners are nominated by teachers for the purpose of recognizing outstanding performance. She was nominated by Mr. Karl Barons from our English Department.

Mr. Barons states, "Erin deserves the Saxon Pride Award because of her daily enthusiasm for life and school, which lights up my third-hour class. Miss Merryn is also very enthused as our Class Act leader and is never afraid to speak her mind. Erin also presented an awesome speech on the nonfiction novel *Alive*, earning an A++. It was one of the best persuasive speeches I have heard in thirty years of teaching. Her poetry collage and explication was also very creative. She is a joy to have in my English class."

The Saxon Pride Program was designed to reinforce good work habits and to single out positive role models for all students. We were proud to recognize Erin as part of this program.

Sincerely,

Sharon E. Cross, Principal

While I realized that I could give a good speech, I needed to start talking more about other things I could never stand up and speak about—the past that consumed me with shame.

Deep down, I was hiding a great deal of emotional pain at a time in my life when I was dealing with flashbacks and nightmares of the sexual abuse I had endured throughout my childhood. I wore a mask to prevent the outside world from knowing the extreme pain I was in. I struggled to talk about the sexual abuse and just wished it would go away and never haunt me again. I had low self-esteem and self-confidence. Before I could move forward, I had to confront my own shame, which stemmed from a past that I still had a hard time uttering a word about to anyone.

There were times when I was prepared and focused while taking an exam and suddenly I would be hit with a flashback. One minute I would be solving $3x + 5 + 2x$, and then suddenly I would be having images of being pushed up against the wall in the shower and assaulted when I was twelve years old. Or I would be in the middle of a history exam, trying to figure out the year that Japan attacked Pearl Harbor and the United States entered World War II, when, like a light switch being turned on, all I could see and feel was me being held down on a couch in the dark, being molested as I hid my face in a cushion so I couldn't see his face. When this happened, I would become so distraught that I would either not write anything down or not even finish the question. These flashbacks severely impacted my poor academic performance on exams.

They didn't just happen while taking exams. They happened at the drop of a hat. I would be in my bedroom doing English homework, and in an instant I would find myself with images of being assaulted in a closet. I could be watching a movie, walking to class, on the telephone, in the shower, or lying in bed trying to fall asleep at night only to toss and turn, feeling the abuse all over again with haunting images.

The psychological impact of childhood sexual abuse is life changing. A child's innocence is killed, their trust of the outside world is forever altered, and the shame and taboo surrounding it make it extremely difficult for a child to talk about, even after they have broken their silence. Without proper and immediate help, a child will be headed for a life of destruction. Most survivors of sexual abuse suffer from post-traumatic stress disorder (PTSD). PTSD is a type of anxiety disorder that many suffer from after a traumatic event, which causes people to relive their trauma through flashbacks and nightmares.

In high school, I was headed down a road of self-destructive behavior. I was so broken inside. So much so that I thought life was not worth living anymore, and, one night, when I was sixteen, I wrote a suicide note to my parents and swallowed a bunch of Tylenol. I remember standing in the bathroom looking at the handful of pills I had in my hands. After swallowing them, I climbed into bed and began crying. I suddenly realized the pain I would put my family through. They had already gone through enough. So, I threw up the pills.

I feared I would spend the rest of my life reliving what Brian did to me through flashbacks and nightmares. In August 2002, I was at our lake house in Lake Geneva, Wisconsin, the same town where my cousin had abused me for the first time. We were part of a private beach association that allowed only members and their guests to have access to the beach. I had swum out to a pier in the water that had a high dive. After twenty minutes, I saw my cousin Brian coming down the pier. He dove off the diving board and was swimming out toward me. I immediately felt trapped and the flashback began. As he swam closer, my memory became clearer.

It was the night we were at a relative's home, and Brian chased me through the house. From one bedroom to another, down two flights of stairs, eventually trapping me in a bathroom, where he pushed me up against the wall and attempted to assault me, but I put up a fight, pushed him off, and escaped.

He continued to pursue me until he trapped me in the pantry. He had that piercing look in his eyes and a big grin on his face. I was fortunate that many of our relatives were in the kitchen, and he couldn't touch me. When he disappeared, I escaped to the basement, where he came searching for me. I was hiding against the washing machine, holding my breath, and praying to God over and over for him not to find me. To my relief, he walked right past me.

Once the flashback ended, I walked home from the lake in tears. As I continued along, I remembered reading about a girl in a teen magazine who cut herself to numb the pain she was in. I decided to try it, a decision I clearly regret making. I began using self-injury the summer of 2002 as a way to be in control of the moments when I could not stop the nightmares and flashbacks. The physical pain of cutting snapped me back into reality and allowed me to have a sense of control over my life.

Most times when a child has been sexually abused, they feel as though their control has been taken from them. Their life then feels chaotic, and at some point in their life—whether as a child or an adult—they seek to reclaim this control. Unfortunately, it is often in unhealthy ways, like self-injury, eating disorders, toxic relationships, addictions, and many other forms of control. Self-injury was just the start of my journey to reclaiming control over my life.

My past was an everyday waking nightmare that I felt I could not escape. I didn't want to talk about it. I tried at different times, but I could only say so much until the shame became too much for me to handle. Shame consumed me, and I constantly felt worthless and dirty inside. It didn't seem acceptable to talk about sexual abuse. It was the unspoken topic, taboo. The shame I carried continued to help me build walls around myself and not reveal the pain I was carrying.

I would often isolate myself, wanting to be alone so nobody could see just how broken I was. My biggest fear was that my past would haunt me forever. I would later learn that we can allow our pasts to haunt us or we can do something about it. The choice is ours. The longer you wait to face your trauma, the more layers you add to the onion you will have to eventually peel away later.

I filled journals with heart-wrenching entries of the horror that I endured and how it followed me wherever I went. Writing was my only outlet as I let my pain pour into words onto each page. It was the only sense of relief I had in a world where I felt so alone, constantly being revisited by my past. It seemed I could not escape the shadow that continued to follow me wherever I went.

The voice of my cousin ran through my mind, "Don't tell anyone. This is our secret. No one will believe you. If you tell them, you will destroy our family."

While I was constantly reliving the abuse from Brian, I was not yet haunted by my earlier abuse. As a child, I had repressed my memories in order to survive. This is something that is so common for survivors of sexual abuse to do. At some point in a survivor's life, those repressed memories surface, and he or she must face them, because ignoring them will only prolong the inevitable—haunting memories through flashbacks and nightmares.

Therapy is a must for a child of sexual abuse. Immediately after my parents learned of the abuse my sister and I endured, my mother was on the phone with a counselor for our family to see. While the support of family is good, a child needs a trained professional with a background in working with survivors of sexual abuse. The abused child might not seem ready to speak about it. This is very common. But it is important for you to keep at it and give the child time. Whether through play therapy for a very young child or cognitive behavior therapy or group therapy for an older child—all important in a child's healing process—they will eventually open up.

The Children's Advocacy Center continued to be there for my family as we moved forward in healing our lives. The center provided individual and group therapy to my family. My parents were in a parent support group together with other parents of sexually abused children. Support groups such as theirs teach parents how to process what their children have gone through, not to blame themselves, how to let go of the guilt, and what to expect as the child or children continue to heal. The center suggested support groups for my sister and me as well. We were both in separate groups for girls that had been sexually abused.

Upon entering a room filled with other girls for the first time, I knew we all had a similar story to tell. We were a part of a group no parent ever wants their child to be a part of, a group of young girls who had experienced sexual violence.

We began with fun icebreakers where we were told to take as many M&Ms as we wanted; what we didn't know was that we had to tell one thing about ourselves for each M&M we took. Confidentiality was covered, of course. We needed this to be a safe environment for all of us. We knew what we shared would not leave the group.

What started off as girls sharing how many siblings they had, their favorite foods, movies, and vacation spots soon progressed into more intimate details of abuse. Of the eight girls, all but one was abused by someone they knew, and yet we had only been educated on stranger danger in school.

One of my parents would drop me and my sister off at the center every week and come back in an hour and a half to pick us up. It wasn't long before I knew I was in a safe environment with these girls. It was the first time since my initial interview that I could talk openly about the flashbacks and nightmares because I had other girls who could relate. It opened the door for me to speak about it in a place where I felt safe and supported. Yet it also paved the way for more flashbacks to occur. However, now it was different. I was in a safe environment with support around me and not suffering in it alone.

Every week, I looked forward to Thursday night's girls group. It was the only time I wasn't alone in my pain. It was much easier to talk there than alone with a therapist. We did trust-building activities, learned about healthy boundaries, worked through the anger and the feelings we had toward our offenders, learned grounding and relaxation techniques for flashbacks, did self-esteem and inner-child work, designed T-shirts, and other therapeutic activities. We also had fun together, and many friendships began to form as a result. I am friends with several of those girls to this day. I even went off to college with one of them, and we have even watched each other get married.

I arrived at the center in April 1998, living in a dark world where I felt alone and terrified as I broke my silence for the first time. Each week that I left the girls group at the Children's Advocacy Center, that dark world I lived in was beginning to get a little brighter as I continued to adapt to life as a survivor of childhood sexual abuse. It was a place where many tears were shed, painful memories revisited, happy, new memories formed, and where a once-silent girl reclaimed her voice. The center ended up being my safe haven, laying the foundation for my healing as I continued to move forward. It prepared me for the weeks, months, and years to come.

Chapter 9

Doubted and Labeled

I HAVEN'T FAILED.
I'VE JUST FOUND 10,000 WAYS
THAT WON'T WORK.

—*Thomas Edison*

I dreaded the last period of my junior year of high school because I ended the day with Algebra 2. It was only a month into the school year and I was already flunking the class because of an exam I had failed. This particular September day was quite difficult. As my teacher went around calling students up to the chalkboard, I sat there hoping I would not hear my name. Maybe if I held my head down and did not make eye contact, she would not call on me.

I held my breath as she called out the names. "John, Mike, Jenny, Sarah, and Erin," she said.

I let out a sigh when I heard my name and nervously walked up to the front of the class. I knew I could start the problem, but I also knew I would just get stuck solving it. Just as before, I could only remember the first few steps in the equation before drawing a blank, something I was accustomed to throughout my childhood. The few students who had been called up completed the equation and took their seats. Just then, I realized I was the only one who had not finished solving the problem. I could feel the piercing gaze from my peers behind me. My teacher was standing across the room by another chalkboard. Clutching the piece of chalk in my hand, I stood there waiting for her to let me sit back down and call upon someone else to finish the equation for me. After what felt like an eternity, my teacher finally spoke, "Erin, do you plan to go to college?"

Surprised at her unexpected query, I responded with a simple yes.

With a very negative tone in her voice, she said, "You need to rethink your plans because you will never get accepted into college. Don't waste your time applying. If you cannot solve algebra equations, you will never get past the admissions test."

My classmates gasped, and there was an eerie silence in the room, with all eyes still fixed on me. I could not believe what I was hearing and felt completely humiliated in front of my peers. In that moment, I wanted to disappear. I didn't say a word. I just hung my head down toward the floor and made my way back to my desk, completely embarrassed and trying not to cry. But it was too late. The tears began welling up in my eyes.

"Now who can go up there and solve the equation for Erin and show her how this is done?" she asked.

Before anyone could volunteer, the bell rang and school was dismissed for the day. I exited as fast as I could and hoped nobody in my class would see that I was crying. Once I was outside the class, I was able to hide myself in the rush of students going to their lockers. I began sobbing to myself as I walked to my locker. "I'm a failure," I said quietly to myself.

With tears still streaming down my face, I grabbed the textbooks I needed for homework out of my locker and headed out to find my mother, who worked at my high school.

"What is wrong?" she asked.

She saw that I was crying, so I proceeded to tell her what had happened in algebra class.

"Your teacher is completely out of line. We are going to straighten this out immediately," she said.

When we arrived at the math department office, the first person to speak with us was a young math teacher who happened to work in the math tutoring office during my free period. She was very familiar with me since I was in there almost daily working with her. When my mother explained to the other math teacher what my teacher had said to me, you could tell by the look on her face that she wanted to have no part in it. She said that my teacher wasn't in her office, but that when she returned, she'd send her out in the hall to speak with us.

I had stopped crying by the time my algebra teacher met with us in the hallway.

"Did you tell my daughter in front of the entire class that she will never get accepted into college and not to bother applying?"

"Yes, I did. Your daughter is failing my class, and, if she can't do algebra in high school, she will never get accepted into college. She needs to hear the truth."

The look on my mother's face said it all. She could not believe what she was hearing and had a look of disgust on her face. My mother said in a very angry tone, "You are supposed to motivate and encourage your students, not crush their self-esteem and bring them down, especially in front of the entire class."

"I am just telling Erin what she needs to hear. Completing all her homework assignments is not going to pass her in my class. She needs to do well on exams, and she has already failed the first one. We are not even past the first quarter, and she is already failing. She would waste her time applying to colleges if she can't do algebra."

I found myself sobbing again as I leaned against a row of lockers, listening while they argued back and forth.

"Why did you feel the need to express your opinion to her in front of the entire class? Why couldn't you talk to her after class? I will not stand here and listen to you continue to humiliate and insult my daughter! I will not let her sit through your class ever again. You are out of line, and I will be speaking to your boss. Come on, Erin. We do not need to hear any more of this!"

I cried the entire walk down the hallway toward the front of the school.

"Erin, she is completely out of line, and I will be speaking to her boss. Do not let her nonsense get to your head. You will get into college and prove her wrong," she emphasized.

"She is right. I will never get into college," I said. "I am stupid and a failure in life. I have always been an academic failure."

"Erin, you know that is not true. Your teacher is way out of line. Do not let her negative comments get to your head. I do not understand how she thinks she can get off saying something so mean and degrading," my mother countered.

I already had a low self-esteem at that time in my life, and my teacher's actions just made me feel even worse about myself. As I walked away from my mom, who had her car parked in staff parking, she turned to me and said, "Erin, we will get this all straightened out. You will get into college."

Before we left school that day, my mother went to set up a meeting with the head of the math department, and I walked into the guidance office where I scheduled an appointment for the following day to see my guidance counselor. After all of this, I planned to drop Algebra 2.

As expected, a pass for me to see my guidance counselor came to my first-class period the next day. I walked into the office and was greeted by the secretary. She always had a kind demeanor and was cheerful to all the students. She called to let my guidance counselor know I was there. Once in my guidance counselor's office, I explained what had happened in algebra class. She then gave me the paperwork to drop the class. She explained to me that I needed to have my algebra teacher fill out the pass/fail agreement form and then my parents and I would need to sign it.

I headed into my eighth-period algebra class the next day for one last time to meet with my teacher. As I walked down the hall toward class, I was filled with anxiety. I could hear the chattering of my peers, but as soon as I walked into the room, their voices fell silent, and all eyes were on me as I approached the front desk and handed her the slip. She signed it and said out loud, "Good luck!" I didn't say anything back.

I was placed in a study hall the last period of the day for the rest of the semester and was scheduled to retake Algebra 2 my senior year of high school with a different teacher. I decided the next semester to retake Algebra 1, which I had already passed my freshman year. I looked at it as a way to refresh my algebra skills.

My mother eventually met with the director of the math department, where she was told that my teacher's statements to me were wrong, but, because she was tenured, there was little he could do other than to write a complaint in her file and have a serious talk with her. I felt she could offer an apology at the very least, but I would never hear one.

The same day that I had gone home crying after being humiliated in front of my algebra class by my teacher, my mom left a message on the school psychologist's voice mail to discuss my academic struggles in school. My mother had watched me all throughout my childhood and teen years as I put forth so much effort, yet I had not displayed the expected results. While the abuse impacted me greatly, we both knew there was more to it than that. Something wasn't right. The thought that something might be going on in my brain that we were not aware of—and that was not allowing me to retain certain information—became very real.

I decided to take matters into my own hands and walked down to the psychology department. When I got there, I noticed that the door to the school psychologist who my mother had left a message with had his door closed, but the other psychologist had her door open, so I nervously walked in.

I introduced myself to Mrs. Ardell and told her briefly before the bell rang that morning about my struggles academically and how it was suggested that I get tested to see if I had an underlying learning disability. She reviewed her schedule to see when she could see me that week during my free period.

I did not know what to expect as I went in to be tested by the school psychologist. I told her how I had put forth so much effort and yet it was not connecting with my ability to retain certain information, especially in math and science, but that I had difficulty in all my other classes as well. I shared with her my background information on my family and how my sisters were both very successful academically.

"My older sister graduated top twenty-five in her class of over six hundred and sixty students. Her junior year she was ranked number one of six hundred and sixty-four students. I envy her. I have always wished I had her ability to do well in school. Both my sisters are in the National Honor Society, and my parents have a proud bumper sticker that reads, 'I have an honor roll student at Schaumburg High School,'" I told her.

Almost instantly, Mrs. Ardell recognized the habit I had begun at a very young age of comparing myself to my sisters, something my eighth grade teacher had encouraged me not to do. I would come to learn not to compare myself to my sisters or peers. I had to focus on myself if I ever wanted to be successful and discover my strengths, not my sisters' strengths.

For the next two months, I continued to get a pass during my lunch or during study hall to see Mrs. Ardell, who did a battery of tests on me through Wechsler Individual Achievement Test (WIAT) and Wide Range Assessment of Memory and Learning (WRAML). All were timed and tested me on oral, reading, listening comprehension, math fluency, problem solving, numerical operations, sentence composition, written language, vocabulary comprehension, letter-numbering sequencing, picture completion, block design, matrix reasoning, and processing speed. I was also evaluated by Verbal IQ (VIQ), Performance IQ (PIQ), and Full Scale IQ (FSIQ). The entire process took weeks to complete.

Many of the tests were cumbersome. At times, I became frustrated, especially during the math portion, which I knew I would struggle with. A variety of equations were thrown at me all at once, from decimals and fractions to algebra. It wasn't all bad though. There was one test that involved having a bunch of words read to me and after Mrs. Ardell finished listing them, I had to repeat as many as I could remember back to her. I recalled nearly every single word, to which I remember Mrs. Ardell being clearly surprised. I took this test back in the fall of 2002, and ten years later, I can still remember items on that list. I was tested with pictures in a similar fashion.

Two months after meeting Mrs. Ardell for the first time, a conference was finally set up to review the results of my tests. I walked into the conference that December afternoon expecting to be told that the tests all came back normal and that maybe I just needed to learn how to relax before an exam and not get so worked up. However, that wasn't the case. Nothing could have prepared me for what I was going to hear.

There were several people in the room, including Mrs. Ardell, the director of the special education department, my mother, the guidance counselor, and one of my general education teachers. After personal introductions were made, the group discussed some background information on the individual case study evaluations that were done on me to explore whether or not there was an underlying learning disability that could explain my academic performance.

Here is what the report entailed:

Academic Performance

I was described by my teachers as a student who works very hard, pays attention in class, completes homework assignments on time, but still seems to fail most of my quizzes and tests. I reported that I wanted to go to a four-year college and become a social worker, but there was some concern that I might not achieve this goal because of my poor test scores, which had significantly impacted my grades.

Records indicated standardized test scores in the areas of reading and written language to be within the average range, while math consistently fell below average compared to my peers.

The math portion of the Wechsler Individual Achievement Test, second edition (WIAT-II) was administered as a part of the evaluation process. Results on the Numerical Reasoning subtest revealed a standard score of 75. This suggested that my ability to solve written math problems fell at about a sixth grade level. I was not surprised as I listened to Mrs. Ardell's remarks. Errors were noted on the test in subtraction and division of multiple digits, as well as fractions. Results of the Math Reasoning subtest revealed a standard score of 80. This suggested that my ability to solve a word or a stated math problem fell within the sixth to eighth grade levels. Areas of difficulty included working with decimals, percentages, and multistep problems. It was noted by Mrs. Ardell in the conference how easily frustrated I became during the math portion of the evaluation with her, which indicated to her that I would probably do poorly.

Communication Status

My speech, language, and communication skills were reviewed and evaluated as part of the case study as well. High school entrance testing indicated that I had average skills in language and reading. It was noted that I did well in language-based classes like history and preschool lab, which was a course where I worked with preschool students teaching them in front of the class. It was also reported that I did well in English. Teachers noted in their evaluation of me that I had excellent pragmatic and interpersonal language communication skills, making me an exemplary leader in leadership, physical education, and preschool teaching.

My positive contributions in my classes showed that interpersonal communication was a strength of mine. Based on my records, current performance, and recent testing done by Mrs. Ardell, the report indicated I had adequate speech/language communication skills for both social and academic success. I did not meet eligibility criteria for speech, language, or communication.

General Intelligence

The Wechsler Adult Intelligence Scale, third edition (WAIS-III) was also administered as part of the evaluation process. According to the results of the FSIQ, I was functioning within the average range of intellectual functioning. My VIQ of 94 and PIQ of 89 indicated that my verbal reasoning and nonverbal reasoning scores were relatively evenly developed. My below-average score on the Picture Completion Subtest reflected a weakness in visual discrimination and perceptual organization. "Erin demonstrates a relative strength in practical knowledge and judgment of social situations," was noted in the evaluation.

My memory was assessed using the Wide Range Assessment of Memory and Learning (WRAML). Results of the WRAML suggested that my visual and verbal memory are relatively evenly developed, each falling within the average range as compared to my same-age peers. It was documented in the evaluation that I demonstrated a relative strength in my ability to recall a list of nonrelated words that were orally presented to me.

Finally, the portion of the conference that I had been waiting to hear the results of arrived. What was to be determined through all those tests? The results were as follows:

☑ Yes ☐ No

A severe discrepancy exists between achievement and ability that is
not correctable without special education and related services.

☑ Yes ☐ No

The team has determined that the eligibility determination is not the
result of environmental, cultural, or economic disadvantage; nor
is it the result of visual, hearing, or motor impairment, emotional
disturbance, or mental retardation.

☑ Yes ☐ No

The student has a specific learning disability.

Specific Learning Disability

The report read: "The IEP team participants determined that the student meets the eligibility criteria for special education services under the
classification of a specific learning disability. The adverse effects upon
Erin's learning include: difficulty differentiating essential from non
essential details, heightened test anxiety, and completing tests and quizzes
at a slower pace."

When I heard the words "learning disability," all I wanted to do
was to get up and walk out of the meeting. I kept telling myself, *They
are wrong. You don't have a learning disability.* This overwhelming
sense of shame came over me. I waited until I was a junior in high
school to finally advocate for myself, and now I was getting an answer
I didn't want to hear. I already possessed the stigma from being sexually abused, and now a learning disability was added on top of it. I
did not want to hear anything else at that point and was getting more
annoyed as they started to talk about the accommodations and goals
they would put in place for me in school, which included placing me

in a resource class for students with a learning disability rather than study hall. The class had a special education teacher in the room and an aide. It was no different than a study hall, other than the fact that the teacher could help each student with schoolwork or administer an exam (with a time extension) from one of the student's classes.

My goals and objectives for the year were as follows:

Goals for 2002–2003

Goal: The student will apply two test-taking strategies.

Objective: Student will learn three test-taking strategies by the end of the third quarter.

Objective: Student will implement two test-taking strategies by the next annual review conference.

Goal: Student will demonstrate independence in the regular education environment.

Objective: Student will independently access supplemental aids and supports in the Resource Service Center as needed.

Objective: Student will pass all courses in the regular education program.

The conference concluded with the team putting accommodations in place that would help me be more successful in school. Now that it was documented that I had a learning disability, I was eligible to receive time extensions on exams, someone to read my exams to me if I chose, and taking exams in a smaller setting rather than my classroom. It was also mentioned that they would add a class to my schedule called "Learning Strategies" the next semester to help strengthen my studying skills, particularly on exams.

A case manager was assigned to meet with me and be available to assist me in making sure I would succeed. Mrs. Ardell knew I was really upset with the news and told me that it was nothing to be ashamed of. As we were getting up to leave the conference, she told me she would be sending a pass to talk later that week about all that had unfolded during the meeting.

According to federal law, a learning disability is a disorder in one or more of the basic psychological processes involved in understanding or using language, spoken or written, which may manifest itself in an imperfect ability to listen, think, speak, read, write, or do mathematical calculations.

Just as I had learned that I wasn't alone in being a survivor of sexual abuse, I also learned that I wasn't alone in having a learning disability. The statistics on individuals who fall into this category are overwhelming, and those who are labeled with it carry a great deal of shame. The National Institutes of Health (NIH) estimates that 17 percent of the population has some type of a learning disability. That means that one out of every five Americans of all ages has some type of learning disability.

- According to the U.S. Department of Education, there are an estimated 4.6 million Americans the age of six and older that have a learning disability.

- According to the National Center for Learning Disabilities, half of secondary students with a learning disability perform more than three grade levels below their enrolled grade in essential academic skills of reading and math.

- Twenty percent of students with learning disabilities drop out of high school compared to 8 percent of the general population.

- Forty percent of students with a learning disability dropped out of high school in 2000. That number dropped to 22 percent in 2009, according to the National Center for Learning Disabilities. The number of students with learning disabilities has been dropping since 2000, but of all disabilities (autism, intellectual disability, speech and language impairments, and other health impairments), the category of learning disabilities still has nearly the highest rate of dropouts, with only emotional disturbance having a higher dropout rate. Studies show that parents' lack of support or doubt that their child with a learning disability could successfully attend college negatively influences the student from pursuing secondary education.

- A 2003 National Longitudinal Transition Study showed that students with learning disabilities who go on to a four-year college are 10 percent of the population compared to 28 percent of those without a learning disability. Disclosing a learning disability to a college is voluntary. Studies show that 52 percent of students who received services for a learning disability in high school did not disclose in college that they had one, which means that they were not given accommodations that may have helped them during their college years. Many students expressed concern about disclosure due to faculty and nondisabled students questioning their accommodations and the stigma that is attached to a learning disability.

- The National Center for Learning Disabilities reports that unemployment is twice the rate for those with a learning disability compared to the general population. Currently, 55 percent of the population with a learning disability is employed compared to 76 percent of the general population.

That night, I disclosed in my journal how the news about my learning disability made me feel. This is what I wrote:

December 16, 2002

And so it has been said after failing hundreds of tests over the past ten years, today they told me in school at a conference I have a learning disability. I am so upset. I was hoping I wouldn't hear those words. I don't want this label. Nobody wants to be told they have a learning disability. Why do I keep getting so many negative labels in my life that carry so much shame? Mom said I should be happy finally finding out what is wrong after all these years and actually having an answer now. She said now I will get the extra help I need. This is nothing to be happy about; it's more like someone telling you that you're stupid and they have proof because it's documented on paper. Next semester they are going to add a special education class into my regular education classes. I don't want that. I don't want to be seen in the special education hallway or classroom. I don't want any of my friends to find out.

I always knew from a young age something wasn't right; it is just hard to swallow the news that it is now on paper, documented as a learning disability. I don't think I will ever want to accept this label. There are the students that get accepted into honor classes or gifted programs and then there are the students that get accepted into a group nobody wants to be in—the group of students accepted into special education classes. I'm already in a group nobody wants to be in. Why another one? God, are you still there? Can you hear me? I just don't get it. Why me? I've suffered through so many traumas in my childhood: medical problems, labeled as behavior disordered as a child, and now as a teen being given the label "learning disability."

I just want to be happy. Is it that difficult to ask for that? I just want some good news. I just want peace in my life. I feel sad, empty, depressed, angry, lost, hurt, stupid, failure, lonely, ashamed, and just tired of this life. I took razor blades to my wrist tonight. I hope one day it all makes sense, because right now it doesn't. I wish I could see where I will be ten years down the road.

Later that week, I sat distressed in Mrs. Ardell's office. She again reminded me that I had nothing to be ashamed of and now I could get the help I needed to succeed. She pointed out that it was a positive thing that we knew what the problem was and that all of my hard efforts were not going unnoticed.

Now that the two months of testing were behind us, it was time to start focusing on the emotional baggage I was ashamed to talk about—the haunting memories of sexual abuse. I felt dirty telling anyone, and I wished the memories would just stop haunting me. I had been hiding my pain through self-injury, which Mrs. Ardell was completely unaware of—that was, until a friend from high school found out and told her. It just happened to be the same day I received my second pass in a week to see Mrs. Ardell.

Because I had already talked to her that week, I was confused about why I was called into her office for a second time. When she confronted me about the cutting in a gentle yet assertive way, my first inclination was to deny it and put my defenses up. As I did, I felt as though she could see right through my lie, so I told her it was true. She asked me to pull up my sleeves, but I refused. She looked at me and reminded me that everything she and I talked about would remain confidential unless I became a harm to myself or others, which I clearly was. She explained that I needed to inform my mom of what I was doing. I began to panic and pleaded with her not to tell. I told her that I would never do it again as long as she didn't tell my mom.

I knew my mother would be very concerned hearing this. I thought I was protecting my parents from seeing me in pain. I did not want them to blame themselves for the abuse I endured. Mrs. Ardell told me she had no choice, she had to. She would be meeting with my mother the next day during my mom's lunch hour. Mrs. Ardell would be sending for me to join the meeting after she met with my mother alone. It was convenient that my mother worked in the same school, but not so convenient for me. I was afraid to face my mother with this news—and of her reaction to it.

I dreaded the next day as the pass came and I made the walk down my high school hallway to the school psychologist's office. As I turned to enter, the first thing I saw was the upset look on my mother's face. I had a hard time looking at her. I felt like I had disappointed her. Looking back on that day, I now understand how difficult it must have been for her to hear that her daughter was taking razor blades to her body. It didn't make sense to my mother, but the physical pain was far more bearable than the emotional pain that haunted me. She didn't understand why I didn't come to her if I was having all these flashbacks but instead chose to inflict pain upon myself. It was hard for her to believe that I had been doing it for more than a year. It was the only way I knew how to cope and still protect my parents from the struggle I was in.

It was decided that I needed to get more help outside of school and see a therapist. I began meeting with a therapist once a week to work on some of the issues surrounding the flashbacks and nightmares I was having that were triggering me to hurt myself. I just wanted someone, anyone, to end my pain. I would often sit in front of the school psychologist or my therapist unable to talk. My voice would go silent in the same way the men that abused me had silenced me. I could not express how deep down the wounded little girl inside me just wanted to scream out about what I had suffered.

I wanted to be heard and not be alone; however, I did not know my way around the pain or how to let anyone in. It was so extremely difficult to get beyond the shame and finally begin to utter the words of what I had endured. I felt so dirty and used.

Mrs. Ardell tried often to remind me that I was now safe. He could not hurt me. She helped work with me on ways to stay grounded if I found myself being pulled into the trauma of abuse.

At this time, I was still carrying the secret of my early childhood abuse, and it wasn't about to come out anytime soon. In therapy, I often put the focus on my academic struggles or on an argument I got into with my sisters or parents, thus avoiding facing the discomfort and pain I carried.

Along with the shame, pain, and confusion, there was a lot of anger and rage I had toward my cousin. I was angry for what he did and how it continued to haunt me. I was angry that what he did had changed my life forever, and I wanted him to feel my pain so badly. I was angry for the loss of relationships I had with his parents and brothers that he stole from me. I had to learn to mourn them and move on. I would eventually learn to address my anger, anger I had had since I was a young child, when my innocence was first taken. It would be my anger that would eventually fuel me into positive action.

I realized that during the end of my junior year of high school, I was taking my anger and pain out on myself through self-injury when I really needed to voice my anger and pain to my cousin. So one night, I did just that. It was a decision that would change the course of my life forever.

Chapter 10

Self-Advocacy

**LIFE IS 10 PERCENT
WHAT HAPPENS TO US
AND 90 PERCENT HOW WE
REACT TO IT.**

—Dennis P. Kimbro

One night, I found myself searching for my cousin's college e-mail address online and was lucky enough to find it. I poured the anger, rage, and pain that I had been bottling up all those years out to him in a raw and revealing five-page letter, which I began with this:

Brian,

This letter is probably coming as a complete surprise to you, but I didn't feel I needed to warn you since you never warned me when you were going to use my body for your own damn pleasures. . . .

Because it was such a harsh letter, I didn't expect a response back. However, I did hear back from Brian a few days later. Here is what he wrote:

Erin,

I know I messed up as a teenager, but God has given me another chance in life, and I am making the best of it. I live my life the best way I know how. I wished what happened never happened and that I could erase it all, but now I accept what I did and I am going to keep on looking to the future and keeping my past as a reminder of my mistakes in life. I don't know what else you want me to say.

Brian

His letter came to me as a complete surprise, and it was the beginning of a seven-month period of correspondence between us. After writing to him about the time when he abused me in his basement under the blankets, he wrote back saying that he never abused me there and only helped hide me during a game of hide-and-seek. Then he tried to convince me that the worst abuse he had ever put me through had been in Wisconsin. He began minimizing his actions, which enraged me greatly. I replied:

> *What!?* I don't know what to say. Listen to yourself, Brian. Can we say "denial"? If you are going to try and tell me that is the only memory you have, then you are in denial. I can't believe you can even say that. My anger is boiling that you could make a comment like that. You're a perpetrator and you know it.

I went on to list a number of other times he abused me, from basements, bedrooms, closets, bathrooms, his garage, living rooms, cars, and so on. I asked him to explain all of them. This was his response:

> Erin,
>
> All this happened in the past, and that is where I wish it could stay. Think of a person you like and respect, and now think if you found out that they did the things I did. That is how I feel about my past. I look at my past as if I was a different person, and I don't want to know anything about him. I don't want to be me at times. That is one of the worst things that someone can say about oneself in life. At least you know you are a good person, Erin. I look at my past and I realize I can't change my past and who I was, and I will never be a good person. Sometimes the best way to live a good life is to forget about my past for a while. Bringing this all back is ripping me apart, and you are probably happy for that, but no matter what you do or say to me, it will not help me look back at my past and forget who I was. Because remembering who I was helps me be the best I can be today and in the future.
> Brian

I wasn't about to let him forget what he did to me, nor was I going to let him skip out on taking accountability for it. Was he really trying to make me feel bad for him by telling me he didn't want to be himself at times? Well, he was the last person I was about to give sympathy to. "Sometimes the best way to live a good life is to forget about my past for a while." While this was easy for him to say, I wish I could forget about my past to this day. Through his letters, I noticed that he often talked only about himself. To me, this revealed just how narcissistic he truly was.

In April 2003, during the same month I confronted my cousin, I was also preparing to take the ACT for college. Because I had a documented learning disability with an individual education plan (IEP), I would be able to take it in a room filled with other students who had an IEP as well, and our allotted time to take the test would be extended. We were also given the option to have someone read the exam to us, which I declined.

The process was long and grueling. I took my time and was glad to be done with it after several hours of testing. I would know the results by the end of May, at which time I would start to begin the research process for college.

I had been placed in a special education class called Learning Strategies for the entire second semester of my junior year. It was a class for students with learning disabilities. It taught us different ways to apply learning strategies in order to be successful in our other classes.

Weeks were spent working on test taking, focusing specifically on the different types of exams, such as multiple-choice, true-false, short answer, and essay, and how to best study for them. I actually felt like this benefited me. The one thing I was happy about was that the class wasn't separated from other classrooms, so when I would be sitting outside class at a desk taking an exam because I needed extended time, nobody would know why. I feared anyone finding out I had a learning disability. It was easy for me not to tell anyone, but it would have been difficult to hide myself if I had been seen in a hallway designated for special education classes only. Luckily, Mrs. Ardell's office was close by, so I could always say I was seeing her as an excuse if need be.

In May, the results of my ACT score came in the mail. After years of harping from my teachers, I knew how important these scores were for getting into college, but I was also aware of my consistent fail pattern on exams, so I did not have high expectations. I knew that to get into some of Illinois's state universities, my score would need to be around 21 or higher, which is what many universities were looking for. However, I also heard that they would take scores of 18–20 into consideration based on other academics over the years.

I opened the ACT envelop that contained my results and read an overall composite score of 16. I could not believe what I was seeing. Was that really a 16? I was hoping for a 19, but a 16? I figured by sitting down, not even reading the questions, and just filling in random multiple-choice answers, anyone could get a 16. *I sat for nearly five hours taking this exam for a score of 16,* I thought to myself. What a waste of time. I feared what this would now mean concerning college. It wasn't like I could hide this information or lie about it. They would clearly see I got a 16 unless I retook it and did better. I decided to make an appointment with my guidance counselor that week to discuss my ACT results and my options for college.

My guidance counselor knew from the day she met me during freshman year that my future plans were to go to college and get a degree in social work, something I had known I wanted to do since I was twelve years old. She was familiar with my struggles in math and had been a part of the two IEP meetings I had. I met with her in her office where she had my file with my grades from the past three years ready in front of her. We began to discuss the results of my ACT and my plans for college.

"Erin, college isn't for everyone, and with your ACT results, grades, and patterns of failing exams, you won't get accepted to a university. You will be wasting your time applying. You would be best finding a job somewhere right out of high school."

Shocked, I sat in silence staring at her as she said this to me. She had known about my plans to go to college for the past three years. The beginning of the year started bad enough with my teacher humiliating me in front of my entire algebra class, which had left me in tears. Now I was hearing my guidance counselor's doubts about me getting into college, and she was trying to discourage me from going. I was now feeling angry. I could not believe what I was hearing. How could she not support me? She hadn't even suggested a junior college. She jumped immediately to working right out of high school.

"Isn't your job supposed to be to encourage your students to go to college, not discourage them and tell them they are wasting their time applying? You certainly are sounding a lot like a math teacher I know."

She pointed out my grades over the past three years of high school, my pattern of low test scores, especially in math and science, and she explained that the ACT score is a huge assessment factor for universities. I felt like she was setting me up for failure, and she could see I was getting really upset. She told me that if I really wanted to go to college, my only choice was a community college, but she felt I would struggle even at a community college.

"College is much different than high school," she said. "There are great jobs out there for students like you right after high school. Not everyone is made for college."

"Yes, the students that are not made for college are the ones who have no desire to go. I have a desire and will go whether you think I will or not! Now, please sign my pass and send me back to class," I snapped back.

She could tell I was fed up with her. I was not going to allow her to hurt my self-esteem anymore. As I exited her office, I said one final thing: "I am sick and tired of people like you who doubt me. I am going to get into college and graduate with a degree in social work. I am not going to let you or anyone else stop me." I was obviously very upset.

While my grades were not the best, I had a lot of determination to accomplish my goals, and I was not going to let anyone prevent me from making that happen. I was fortunate enough to have a school psychologist who helped encourage me and assist in building up my self-esteem. When she heard the negative messages I was getting, she continued to say to me repeatedly, "Erin, you will get into college. Don't let anyone stop you."

I took action and made an appointment with the director of student services to request a new guidance counselor. My parents saw how upset I was, and they reassured me that I would get into college, even if it meant starting off at a community college and transferring.

For forty-five minutes, I explained to the director of student services that my goal since I was twelve years old was to go to college and get a degree in social work. I shared with him what happened in algebra class at the start of the year and how the year was ending with what my guidance counselor had said to me.

"Teachers and guidance counselors are supposed to support and encourage students to go on to college, and instead, I'm hearing the complete opposite, with adults doubting my success, humiliating me, and crushing my self-esteem," I said to him.

Apologizing for both their behaviors, he explained that both my teacher and guidance counselor were wrong and that no student deserves to be treated that way. He was very proud that I took matters into my own hands and came to him with it.

I shared how much effort I put toward school and how I struggled on exams in many of my classes. I explained how it had been this way my entire life and how frustrating it was to know your teachers think you are not applying yourself when you are. Then you see the student that ditches class all the time or never completes their homework assignments and shows up only on exam days and ends up acing them and doing better in the class than me. In utter frustration, I then disclosed my learning disability to him.

"I am not going to let a learning disability or any adult stop me from pursuing my dreams!" I exclaimed.

"Keep that attitude and you will do it," he said.

He went on to describe how he had a son who struggled in some areas of school, including math, and despite this, he got into a great college called Western Illinois University (WIU). He explained how his son was doing better in college than he had in high school and how he felt that there was a college out there to fit everyone. "As long as you apply yourself, you can make it happen," he said. He knew I no longer wanted to work with my guidance counselor and supported me on that decision. He told me he was going to switch my counselor for the rest of high school. I thanked him and stated how much I appreciated his support.

I knew in my heart that as long as I applied myself, I could get it done, and I have proved it. Not only did I go on to get a degree in social work, but I became a writer, which began as a year-long writing assignment in sixth grade. My goal was to make both dreams a reality. I was not about to give up on either, no matter what anyone told me. I was determined to overcome any obstacle placed in front of me by accomplishing everything I went after. With the right attitude and determination, you, too, can accomplish all that you want to achieve, no matter what others may think. I am living proof.

Chapter 11

Forgiving and Planning a Future

FORGIVING DOES NOT ERASE THE
BITTER PAST. A HEALED MEMORY IS NOT
A DELETED MEMORY. INSTEAD,
FORGIVING WHAT WE CANNOT FORGET
CREATES A NEW WAY TO REMEMBER.
WE CHANGE THE MEMORY OF OUR PAST
INTO A HOPE FOR OUR FUTURE.

—*Lewis B. Smedes*

S oon I had another year of high school behind me. While it was going by fast, there were days that seemed so slow. Those were the days when the pain I carried alone consumed me the most. While there was so much darkness, I slowly began to realize that we are in control of our own happiness. I could choose to stay miserable and ashamed, or I could do something about it. I woke up one day and realized that every day I stayed unhappy, I was allowing the person who caused me pain to take yet another day of my joy. He already took so much from me. I couldn't give anymore. I just didn't have the answer to solve this dilemma yet, but I soon would.

The summer before my senior year of high school, I got an idea to turn my childhood diary into a book as a way of putting a face and voice to the silent epidemic of child sexual abuse and, in turn, learn to let go of the shame. I began by looking up the statistics of sexual abuse survivors. I was stunned to see how many people are affected by sexual abuse. One in four girls and one in six boys will be molested before their eighteenth birthday. As I thought about these numbers, I realized that there could be someone sitting next to me in English class who had endured the same pain I did. I felt like a light had been turned on, and I suddenly realized that I could do something huge by stepping out into the public eye and declaring that I had been sexually abused and that I had nothing to be ashamed of, and neither had anyone else who had survived abuse.

I was just as determined to get a book published as I was to get into college. I poured hundreds of hours into my diaries from my childhood and teen years. I began marking the pages that I wanted to share, which I felt would best relay the secrets I kept, the healing I found, and the silence that needed to be shattered. I sat at a computer for hours every day typing word for word what I had written in diary entries over the course of the summer. I didn't tell anyone what I was doing. I figured, like so many people in my life, I would be doubted and discouraged.

The start of my senior year began shortly after. I was retaking Algebra 2, which I had withdrawn from the year before after my teacher humiliated me in front of my entire class. I was going to math tutoring every day and taking my exams with time extensions this time around. Despite these adjustments, I soon found myself in the same predicament I was in the year prior. I was failing. I would do well with my math tutor present but, as soon as it was time to take an exam on my own, I would not be able to complete the problems. At times, I just wanted to bang my head against the desk in utter frustration because my effort didn't show.

I had an excellent teacher and soon began to joke with him, saying, "This is my second attempt at Algebra 2 and I am failing again. I guess it is time to start filling out the McDonald's application." Unlike my previous math teacher, he continued to encourage me not to give up and stated that with determination, I would be successful. When I failed another exam, I actually arrived to class the next day with a McDonald's application and told him that I was ready to ask people the rest of my life, "Do you want fries with that?" I got a great laugh out of him. And, at the very least, I was showing my sense of humor during frustrating times.

I cannot describe the frustration I felt at my second attempt to pass Algebra 2. I poured so many hours into trying to pass even with just a D, and I couldn't even pull that off. Soon I was forced to withdraw from the class once again and placed in the resource room to ride out the rest of the semester. At least I knew I was giving it my all, and many could see that. While the letter grade matters to college admissions, what truly mattered to me was my determination.

Not only was I struggling in algebra, but I also had a lot of emotional pain from my past that was screaming for my attention. I still experienced flashbacks, nightmares, and panic attacks. Despite this, I was still e-mailing my cousin. While I was forcing myself to relive so many terrible memories by confronting him, it was also empowering writing the letters and letting him hear the voice he silenced.

Despite the progress I had made, I was still taking razor blades to my wrists. Confronting my cousin stirred up a lot of emotions inside me that I had not addressed. There was another secret buried that I carried deep inside me that was so terrible I didn't even want to believe it myself, and I had always assumed that I would never tell anyone. I remember sitting across from Mrs. Ardell one afternoon as she tried to get me to talk about what was on my mind. I couldn't do it. She didn't know what had happened when I was little. Nobody knew that other secret, and as I sat there replaying the assault in my mind, I just couldn't share it with anyone.

I remember taking an exam in physical education class my junior year when suddenly a flashback came over me. My PE teacher took notice and even asked what was wrong. I couldn't tell her and told her not to worry. Instead, I found myself in a bathroom cutting.

One day while sitting in the only special education class I had that year, which was Learning Strategies 2, I had a terrible flashback that nearly consumed me. Usually I could hide it from others by using self-injury or other healthier grounding techniques I had learned in therapy. This day was different. I couldn't hide it, and my classmates noticed and notified the teacher. She immediately stopped teaching and tried to get me to talk. I couldn't get the words to come out of my mouth. I was trapped in a horrible memory. I tried so hard to say something but was unable to speak.

That was a day I will never forget. I was eventually moved from the guidance office to the nurse's office where they left me curled up on a bed in a dark room with the door closed. The memory continued to flood my mind, and I just cried. I felt so alone in my horror in that dark room. Darkness fueled my flashbacks because so much of my abuse happened with the lights off or at night in some enclosed area. I remember crying out to God, pleading with him.

"You are the only one who can see exactly what I am going through daily. Please hear me and make it stop. Help me! I will do anything— just show me what I need to do. I am begging you, God!" I wanted so badly to take razors to my wrists right then and there, but I left all my stuff in class.

Mrs. Ardell was notified after getting out of a meeting and soon rushed to the nurse's office to find me in the dark room. She sat next to me, comforting me and telling me repeatedly that I was safe. She tried getting me to talk but I couldn't pull myself out of the flashback. She eventually went to find my mother. When they both returned, they thought giving me ice-cold water would help, which it did. It was a grounding technique I had heard about before. I sat up eventually and said, "I can't keep living like this." The two of them made a call in the nurse's office to my therapist, at which point it was determined that I needed to see my psychiatrist immediately.

I left school early that day with my mom. I was seen by my psychiatrist the next day and then sent directly to the behavioral health hospital for an assessment. Shortly afterward, I was admitted to the Partial Hospitalization Program, where I would spend all day at the hospital but still be able to go home at night to sleep in my own bed. At first, I was resistant to the idea of being in the hospital, because it would just be another label that carried shame with it. As I was about to enter this hospital, all I could think about were the movies *One Flew Over the Cuckoo's Nest* and *Girl Interrupted.*

I was put on new medication called Risperdal to deal with the panic attacks and intrusive memories. I was already taking an antidepressant and sleep medication, and now medicine to deal with my thought process. I learned many skills to help ground myself when having flashbacks and nightmares while in the program. I wanted more than anything to be able to help the other patients in the hospital with their problems. I often gave suggestions to them when they were processing things. The therapists pointed out to me a few times that I gave great feedback to other patients. It was that social worker inside me that I dreamed of becoming. In part, it also was a way to avoid dealing with my own issues.

The program at the hospital was only during the week, so I was allowed to go home during the two weekends that fell within the program. It just so happened that the Chicago Marathon was the weekend following the week I was admitted to the hospital. So what does the Chicago Marathon have to do with my breakdown? I had agreed to participate on behalf of the Children's Advocacy Center back in the spring. I raised $1,000 for the center by having people pledge money to me for taking part in the run. I was not going to let my mental state of mind stop me. I was determined to go out there and do it no matter how long it took me. I would finish knowing that each step I took was for the children that had been abused. I knew that the people who pledged for me to do the marathon would have understood my situation if they knew, but accomplishing this was more about stepping forward in my own recovery. I crossed the finish line of the Chicago Marathon that weekend, proving to myself that no matter how large the obstacle might seem, it could be overcome.

A month after my discharge from the hospital, a letter arrived from my cousin. This is what it said:

November 2003

Erin,

I would assume that if you never forgive me for my actions that over time you will build this hate and this rage would in turn spark a need or want for revenge. I do not know if this would happen, but I do know that if it did it would consume your life and mine. All I want is for all of us to go on living a much happier life, as well as a more satisfying one. I know that when you get a thought of me it probably consumes your thoughts and feelings for a long extent because when I used to hear your name or if I was talking to someone about my cousins, my thoughts and emotions would rip into me for more than a day because I really felt that I had messed up your life as well as mine. I pray that someday this feeling goes away. I hope one day that I feel satisfied enough that I haven't destroyed the rest of your life. I believe that will only come when you have accepted my apology.

Erin, I am sorry for what I did to you. My actions weren't thought out, I was confused and disoriented, and I acted on the behalf of just plain stupidity. I wish that I had never hurt you the way I did. I wish I could go back into my past and stop myself and teach myself what was wrong with my actions, but I had to learn the hard way, and unfortunately you were the one I abused. I apologize for the past and I hope that you can forgive me, but if you can't, I understand. I am sorry.

Brian

I read it over and over again, possibly more than twenty times that night. I realized that how I responded was my decision to make. It was through reading his letter that I realized that I was the one who allowed him to continue to rob me of my happiness every day by continuing to hate him. The bitterness, anger, and pain I felt consumed me. I could continue to allow it to consume me, but what good would that do? Why let the person who hurt me so much continue to take another day of my happiness?

What he did in the past hurt me, but I had to take control and stop allowing his past actions to hurt me in the present. His letter gave me a moment of reflection and clarity. I realized that I also needed to forgive myself before I could forgive him.

While I didn't choose to be abused, I did have a choice on how to deal with it. I was not responsible for the sexual abuse. I wasn't responsible for my sister being abused. I was responsible for how I allowed it to affect my life. By the age of seventeen, I had been choosing to respond to my past in a very self-destructive way, and each day I spent consumed in the pain was another day of my life taken away from me. Another day I could not get back.

I had so much anger and hatred for my cousin. For many years, I wished for terrible things to happen to him. I was wishing this for someone I once loved and trusted, someone I had once looked up to as a brother. I was so mad at him for taking the good person I knew in him away from me. He betrayed me in the worst possible way and stole my innocence.

What I didn't realize at the time was just how much of my life I had allowed to be consumed by this pain and anger. It wasn't going to go away. I knew that. Unlike a really bad headache where you can take ibuprofen to make it go away, there was nothing I could take to change the past or get rid of the images that haunted me. I would give anything for my mind to forget about it. If my past was an exam and I had to give a play-by-play of what happened from the first day I was abused by Ashley's uncle to the last assault from Brian, I would ace it. I had to find a way to accept the past for what it was and to find a way to not let it impact me in a negative way anymore. I was about to discover the answer I had been looking for all along.

The decision I need to make is, do I offer him grace and forgiveness? I asked myself. Forgiveness is a gift we give ourselves to the ones who hurt us. No matter what the circumstances, we can choose to hate our enemies and continue to allow them to take our happiness or we can forgive them and learn how not to allow the pain to destroy the rest of our lives. Anger and hatred can consume so much of our lives, but what good does it serve?

I made a decision that is extremely difficult to make for anyone who has been hurt the way I was. I chose to forgive my cousin. My strong faith in God helped me with this. God's guidance led me to this place of peace. My cousin gave in to temptation and committed a terrible crime that he doesn't deny. That doesn't mean he was deserving of my forgiveness for what he did to me. Forgiving him allowed me to find courage and strength inside myself that I never knew existed. It was November 22, 2003, and I was opening up a new chapter in my life, one not filled with anger, hatred, or shame, but of joy, peace, and forgiveness instead.

When you forgive, you discover that you have been a prisoner inside yourself all along, waiting to be set free from the pain that has robbed you of so much of your happiness. Are you going to allow the pain in your life to take another day away from you? Are you going to continue to be a prisoner? You are the only one who holds the keys to set yourself free. Why should you be punished for someone else's actions? You're not benefiting from staying angry and bitter. You're only hurting yourself. This is what forgiveness has taught me.

I wish they offered a class in high school or college called "Forgiveness." I think it would help so many people live happier lives. Maybe forgiving those who initially confined you in the first place is a necessary step to release yourself from your personal prison. The peace and freedom you will unveil will be rewarding. I promise you will benefit from it and live a better life. The choice is ultimately yours. Nobody can do it for you.

A diary that began with talking about lemonade stands, playing with dolls, and birthday parties, and eventually evolved into keeping the secrets of my abuse, was ready to be published. I finished the last chapter on the message of forgiveness, a topic that I hadn't seen coming. For me, it wasn't an ending; it was a new beginning.

Now, I just needed to find a publisher. Who gets published when they are a senior in high school, especially on a topic that is graphic and disturbing at times and on a subject society rarely talks about and perceives as taboo? Well, if you haven't figured out by now, I am one determined woman, and I make things happen. I was not going to let anything or anyone stop me. I learned to embrace any roadblock that came my way by finding a way around or over it.

I didn't really know anything about the publishing process or how to go about it. I just took a wild leap and went for it. I sent sample chapters to several publishers, including Health Communications Inc. (HCI). I was familiar with the company because of their previously published books *Chicken Soup for the Soul* and *A Child Called It*, both perennial bestsellers. Exactly a month after forgiving my cousin, I received a letter back from HCI. I remember being excited just to be getting a response back from a publisher; it meant they read the sample chapters I had sent. I still have that letter to this day. It read:

December 11, 2003

Dear Erin Merryn,

Thank you for the opportunity to review your manuscript. After a careful review, we decided to pass on this. With the exception of the Dave Pelzer books, we have not done very well in our general market with this type of book. This is purely a business decision, which in no way reflects on the quality of your work.

Thank you for thinking of Health Communications.

Sincerely,

The Editors

I was not surprised and soon received other letters from publishers very similar to this. Some didn't even respond. I wouldn't let these rejection letters stop me in my mission to put a face and voice on sexual abuse and get my diary published. I have read all of Dave Pelzer's books and they are very powerful, especially *A Child Called It*. The difference, though, was that Dave Pelzer's books were on physical abuse. He did an exceptional job at putting a face and voice to a little boy who was tortured. I wanted to paint a similar picture of the girl I was who had endured years of sexual abuse in order to give others courage to step out of their darkness and shame.

At the same time I was receiving rejection letters from publishing companies, the college in Wisconsin that I really wanted to go to responded to my admissions application. It was a letter telling me I was not accepted. When I saw the words "denied admissions," I immediately remembered what my math teacher said to me a year earlier about never getting accepted into college. I thought that with a documented learning disability, I would get accepted. I thought it would be the one thing that benefited me, despite my poor grades.

However, it wasn't working out that way. I decided that giving up was not an option; I wouldn't let it be. There had to be a way for me to accomplish my goal of getting accepted into a university.

I was going to find a way to go away to college like I had planned all along. These rejection letters from publishers and colleges were nothing but pieces of paper in my eyes. I knew what I was capable of, and I had my heart set on accomplishing what I had envisioned ahead of me. I was going to continue to be persistent. Many in my shoes would have given up. I thought about Western Illinois University, the college that the director of student services at my high school had told me about. Seeing no alternative options, I applied.

Despite the rejections I was receiving, I found something in myself: confidence, determination, perseverance, and drive. I had to keep a positive attitude. I wasted too many years living life with a bad attitude, in pain, and carrying shame. It was time to get moving, shatter the silence, and pursue my goals.

I eventually heard about self-publishing and began researching self-publishing companies. While it would cost several hundred dollars to get self-published, it was worth the price to shed light on the pain and devastation caused by sexual abuse and to give those in silence a voice, a voice I didn't have throughout my childhood and adolescence. You could not put a price tag on what happened to me as a child nor my decision to go public. The price to get published cost me in more ways than one. But I knew it would be worth it, and I convinced myself that I would have no regrets because I had nothing to be ashamed of. I have a voice, which I plan to use to shatter this silent epidemic until my very last breath on earth.

Chapter 12

Turning Dreams into a Reality

BELIEVE YOU CAN
AND YOU'RE HALFWAY THERE.

—*Theodore Roosevelt*

From the tender age of seven, I wanted to grow up to become a writer. I discovered the confidence in me I was searching for all along. We all have confidence; you just have to dig deep and start believing in yourself. You are not going to find the answers in a textbook, but you will in your heart. I believed that I would get my diary published no matter what. I made that dream a reality in my final semester of high school. I became a published author when my self-published book *Stolen Innocence* was released in March 2004.

Secrets that I once kept locked away were now available to anyone who wanted to read them. However, this book only confronted the abuse in my life from my cousin. I was at a point in my life where I was not yet ready to revisit the darker chapters of my past and reveal all of my secrets. I had shared the parts of my life from ages ten through high school with the world. I needed to find the courage to face the abuse I had endured that started at six years old, courage that I would find later in my life.

There is a time and place for everything, and it wasn't yet time for me to share those chapters. One thing was for sure, I was turning my dreams into reality, and, for once in my life, I felt I had something outside of perfect attendance to be proud of. I believed in myself. While I had men who took my voice, which I had now reclaimed, and adults who doubted me, I was proving to myself that anything is possible as long as you continue to believe in yourself. I was turning tragedy into triumph, and I was just getting started.

When I was just about to graduate high school and still had not heard back from Western Illinois University, I decided to write to the admissions department to see if they had made a decision. This was their reply:

May 25, 2004

Hello Erin,

We did review your application for admission and I'm sorry to tell you that you will be receiving a deny letter. We were very impressed with your determination and with how you have turned an incredibly traumatic event into something positive. We hope you will continue your education at a community college for two semesters and then transfer to WIU as a sophomore. If you complete twenty-four semester hours of transferrable credits and achieve a C average, you will be automatically admitted as a transfer student. Your ACT and high school grades no longer enter into an admission decision at that point.

When we deny a student, we do so because we honestly feel the student would be best served strengthening his or her academic base before attending a four-year institution. We don't want students to come and struggle academically when another year building a more solid academic base elsewhere would increase their chances of success here. You would not lose any time on a degree because you would be taking general education courses during the first two semesters and these would transfer and count as classes here. I would even be happy to help you select courses if you let me know the name of the community college you would attend. We really want you to keep Western in your future—we just want you to become a stronger student before you come. Please let me know if I can help you in any way.

Candace McLaughlin
Director, UAASC

It was no surprise to me by now, since I was used to being denied. I called a friend who was in her first year of college at WIU, and she told me about some students who lived in her campus dorms who had attended the local community college in town. I decided to research a community college in Macomb, Illinois, called Spoon River, which was exactly four hours from home. I had a great community college just a few miles from my hometown, but I wanted to get away and experience life outside the town I grew up in.

I decided to go for it. I went down to the community college and took some placement tests for classes, met with an admissions counselor, and went to the housing department at WIU to fill out the paperwork for housing. I was excited about the opportunity to experience a new town and be away from home.

I was glad to have high school behind me. My parents made the four-hour drive with me to the small town of Macomb, Illinois, where I would spend the next four years of my life. I went from living in a town of nearly 80,000 people with one of the biggest malls in America to a small town of 20,000 surrounded by cornfields. The majority of the population was college students. My schedule my first semester included English, Speech, Psychology, Government, and Algebra 2. Here I was again, for the third time, taking Algebra 2. I had to have a positive attitude and thought that maybe I would find success a third time. By success, I was just hoping to pass with a C because I knew I needed that to get accepted into WIU the next year.

A good professor can make all the difference in how successful you are in a class. I would soon come to realize how lucky I was. I felt like I landed the best teacher possible to assist me in passing algebra. It was like the class was designed just for me. The teacher's name was Mr. Shepard. He was a wonderful man who really was dedicated to his job and the success of his students. If you didn't understand something, he went to great lengths to help you. I started my day off with algebra. It was a good thing that I was a morning person. It also helped me in not dreading the rest of the day. If I had an exam in algebra, I could get it done and over with first thing in the morning. In high school, it always seemed to be the class I ended with.

Right before an exam, Mr. Shepard would review the material by doing examples on the board, very similar to high school when I had a math tutor. If I had an example in front of me, I could usually figure out the equation. Mr. Shepard never erased the practice equations from the whiteboard, so I had an example to look at while taking the exam. I thought maybe it would only happen once, but before every exam he reviewed with us and left it on the whiteboard.

I found myself acing every one of his exams. The class I had failed twice I was now getting an A in, all because I had an example of the equation on the board. I felt so blessed to be in his class. The high school girl who once dreaded hearing her name called to the board to solve an equation was now willing to jump out of her seat to solve the problem or to give an answer. Mr. Shepard had no idea how much I had struggled in high school, but, in his class, he saw me as a standout student and called on me all the time. He even asked if I would come in early before class and help the girl who sat next to me who didn't understand the material. Who would've thought?

I was doing well in all my other classes, too, and when it came time for semester grades, I received straight A's. Not only did I pursue going to college, for the first time in my life I wasn't failing. I did it for myself and myself only. I knew that if I didn't give up, my hard work would eventually pay off. All the tears and frustration over the years helped mold me into the person I had become.

As a freshman in college, I chose to reach out to HCI again to see if I could get them to reconsider, and they did just that. It's amazing what can happen if you never give up on your goals and dreams, isn't it?

I was also accepted into WIU after one year at the community college. The only real difference was the location of my classes and being able to walk to class rather than drive to the local community college. To my delight, my younger sister began attending classes there too.

During my final semester of high school, I had been informed that because I had a documented learning disability, I would be allowed special services in college similar to those I had received in high school. However, I made the choice not to make the university aware of my learning disability. Since I went most of my life with a learning disability that was undocumented and had made it through, I knew I could accomplish what I was going after if I just continued to believe in myself. While I had a habit of being one not to seek help in the past in many areas of my life due to shame and pride, this was different. This time I chose to keep my learning disability private due to the confidence I had in myself, and I believed that I would be successful at finishing college all on my own.

I transferred to the university with a major in social work and minor in psychology. For the next three years, I was right on track to graduate. I was accepted into the Honors Social Work Society, and I knew I wanted to go on and get my master's degree. Therefore, I began looking for a university to attend and eventually applied to Aurora University, a small private university in the western suburbs of Chicago.

On December 20, 2007, I received a letter congratulating me on getting accepted into the advance standing master's program. I was thrilled knowing I got into grad school, but I knew I could do it. I would be the first in my family to get a master's degree. The drive in me to accomplish this helped me get to this point. I knew that the moment I crossed the stage to receive my master's degree would be priceless, a moment that many doubted I would ever accomplish.

Because I would be graduating with an undergrad in social work, I was admitted into an advance standing program where I could finish my master's in a year instead of two or three. I decided to focus my studies on school social work. It would involve going to school full-time and doing an internship part-time in a school three days a week working with students.

My final semester as an undergrad was spent in an internship working in a domestic violence and homeless shelter for women and children in crisis. It was called Community Crisis Center. Unbeknownst to me, as I was stepping into this role just months away from accomplishing my goal of graduating college, a crisis would occur in my own life.

You can blink, and, in a moment, your life can change forever. I've blinked and have had that happen several times before. It was about to happen once again, and nothing could have prepared me for what would happen next.

Chapter 13

Life Changing

**THAT WHICH DOESN'T KILL US
MAKES US STRONGER.**

—*Friedrich Nietzsche*

I t was a cold, sunny January afternoon in 2008. It was nearly one o'clock as I came upon a busy intersection. The light had just turned red and I made my way into the left turn lane, putting my foot on the brake.

Without warning, an awful sensation suddenly came over me. It felt like everything was going in slow motion. Feeling like I was about to faint, I began tilting my head back and forth. My airway began to feel like it was being cut off, and I needed air. I remember rolling down the window and saying out loud, "What is happening to me?" My voice sounded so faint, like it was miles away. "I need air. I cannot breathe," I gasped. Moments later, I saw this bright, white light appear. That was the last thing I remembered. In that moment, I thought I was seeing the light and crossing over into heaven.

When I woke up, I was certainly not in heaven—far from it. It was more like hell on earth. I actually thought I was in a nightmare, wanting desperately to be woken. I was in the back of an ambulance with three paramedics surrounding me, one man taking my blood pressure, another man asking my name, and a woman who appeared in my line of vision. I was in a complete state of confusion and panic. "What happened to me? Where am I?" I asked. But they did not answer. In a sense, it felt a lot like how I felt as a child when I would wake up to find myself being sexually abused, not knowing what was going on and not having any control over the situation.

One of the male paramedics asked, "What day is it?"

"Wednesday," I replied

"Try again."

"I don't know."

"Where were you coming from?"

"I don't know. What happened to me? Please, tell me what happened."

The back doors to the ambulance were open, and I could see cars on the busy intersection passing by.

The female paramedic finally answered me. "You've been in an accident. You had a seizure." She asked if I had any seizure-related conditions.

I was so confused and disoriented, and kept asking them to let me go home.

"Honey, we need to take you to the hospital and get you checked out," one of the paramedics responded.

As I became more aware of my surroundings, I noticed my pants were soaking wet.

One of the male paramedics who was talking to a police officer came back into the ambulance and noticed me looking down at my pants. "Oh, did you pee your pants?" he asked. It was really more of a statement than a question.

Now I was ready for God to wake me up from this nightmare. Not only was I completely confused, but now I was mortified as well. I pulled my phone out of my pocket and dialed my mom's cell number. She picked up on the first ring. I began crying. "Mom, I don't know what happened. I am so confused."

She panicked, of course. I handed the phone to the female paramedic who could explain what had happened better than I could. I listened intently as she told my mother that I had hit the man in front of me because I'd had a seizure at the wheel. The man I hit had looked up in his rearview mirror and saw me violently shaking. He jumped from his car and came to my aid. He reached over to put my car in park and called 911. He said that from the time he reached me until the point I stopped shaking seemed to be about thirty seconds.

When my parents arrived at the scene, they expected to see my car smashed up. But since I was at a stoplight with my foot on the brake when the seizure began, I had rolled into the car in front of me, only tapping it. Neither car had a scratch on it.

When I entered the emergency room, I was crying, confused, and wondering why this had happened to me. I went through a number of tests over the next seven hours. I had an EKG and a CT scan of my brain. We could not understand why I'd had a seizure when I had never had one before. Was it because I was worn out from the stress of my intense, weeklong training or staying up too late the night before?

The doctor said all the tests came back fine so he discharged me with the follow-up to see a neurologist. I was ordered not to drive until I was cleared by a neurologist. He gave me the name of one with instructions to call him in the morning to set up an appointment.

I woke up the next morning and every muscle in my body ached. I was in so much pain. It felt like every muscle had been pulled. The seizure gave them the biggest workout they had ever had. Every little movement hurt, and I had a headache that lasted for days.

I met with the neurologist five days later. After getting a full medical history from me, he concluded that the seizure must've occurred due to a lack of sleep or stress. He needed to make sure everything was physically okay with me though, so he ordered me to get an EEG of my brain and also for me to meet with a heart doctor. He told me not to drive until all tests came back normal. He explained that most people are not cleared to drive for the first six months after having a seizure. Just the thought of that made me want to cry. Not only did I feel that I had lost complete control of my life, but I also lost my independence.

So much of my life changed after that seizure. January 12, 2008, had a completely new meaning to me. I began looking at life in an entirely new light. Anxiety and fear about having another seizure haunted me. I began to think, *if this can happen, then what else could happen?* So many thoughts that I had never thought of before raced through my head.

A few weeks after the seizure, my sister drove me to the neurologist to get the EEG results of my brain. It was a sleep-deprivation test. I had to stay up most of the night, limited to two or three hours of sleep. The next morning, I went into the doctor's office where a medical technician attached wires to my head. The wires measured my brain's electrical activity. This test would show if there was any spiking or firing activity in the brain. The process took more than an hour.

I knew by the look on the doctor's face as he walked in that the results were not good. It was that look that says, "I have life-changing news for you." He closed the door.

"Your EEG and MRI both show problems in your temporal lobe. It's called mesial temporal lobe sclerosis."

Confusion and panic enveloped me. What he had said was a bunch of foreign nonsense to me. "What is it? What does that mean?"

"You have temporal lobe epilepsy," he replied.

My head started spinning. "That can't be right. How is this possible? This cannot be happening to me!" Tears soon filled my eyes. I didn't want to believe what I was being told. I was completely unprepared for this diagnosis.

The neurologist spent the next twenty minutes explaining that I would need to take seizure medication for life, I would not be able to drive for six months from the day of the seizure, and the best treatment option would be brain surgery. "You most likely developed this kind of epilepsy when you were coming out of the birth canal."

Sitting there in the doctor's office, I became overwhelmed hearing all of this and began crying hysterically. I walked in that morning with the impression that I had had a seizure due to too much stress, and I walked out knowing it was epilepsy. The neurologist made the diagnosis even worse by warning me about the birth defects that my medication could cause. It only made me cry more. I was not at a point in my life to start a family, but with him telling me I would need to be on medication for life, it meant that, at some point, this would be a cause for concern.

He gave me several sample boxes of Lamictal and a prescription for it. Lamictal is used to treat focal seizures, primary and secondary tonic-clonic seizures, and seizures associated with Lennox-Gastaut syndrome. It is also commonly known for treating bipolar disorder. I had an appointment to see him in a month. I could not even talk to the woman booking the appointment as I stood in front of her. I was crying so hard. I didn't even stop in the waiting room where my sister Caitlin had been waiting for me. Seeing that I was distraught as I raced on by, she managed to finally catch up to me outside and asked what happened.

The entire way home I kept telling her how I could not handle any more pain and confusion in my life. I felt defeated, weak. What control I had been taking back seemed to be ripped away from me in an instant. I had just been given a new label that I once again had no control over. I rested my head against the window and sobbed as I said, "I have only so much strength. My heart cannot carry more pain. I cannot handle another hurdle. I can't do this anymore."

She reached over and held my hand. "Erin, look how much you've overcome. Yes, this is a blow, but you can rise above this, too."

At the time, I couldn't connect with what she was saying. I felt that it was easy for her to say because she wasn't the one with epilepsy.

"I don't have the energy to find meaning behind all this pain. I've done enough of that. I just want to give up on life."

I spent the rest of the day lying on the couch and crying. So much uncertainty ran through me. I feared I would spend the rest of my life worrying if and when I would have another seizure, how frequently they might occur, and if I would ever get my independence back.

My mother left work early that day after hearing the news and called Nancy, a good family friend whose daughter has epilepsy and works with some of the best doctors in the state of Illinois at the Epilepsy Center at Rush Hospital in Chicago. Nancy has dedicated her life to epilepsy because of how it has personally affected her entire family. I always felt so much compassion for Nancy's daughter, Megan, whose life has faced so many challenges as a result of epilepsy. They have come so close to losing her. My mom, sisters, and I attended mud volleyball fund-raisers for epilepsy awareness to recognize Megan for a few years. Little did I realize at the time how much it would affect my own life. Nancy recommended Megan's doctor. She was able to set up an appointment for me to see Dr. Marvin Rossi, a specialist in epileptic disorders.

By mid-February, just a few weeks after I received the diagnosis of epilepsy, I received a second opinion from Dr. Rossi. After reviewing my medical history, MRI, and EEG, he questioned the diagnosis. He stated that you have to have two or more seizures to be given that diagnosis. It was bittersweet news.

I was eventually admitted to the hospital by Dr. Rossi in Chicago to run better tests. I was having terrible side effects from Lamictal, including intense headaches, which were rare for me before that. He placed me on Topamax, another antiseizure medication. Within a day of taking it, my head was spinning. It didn't matter if I stood up or lied down, I had a constant spinning feeling. It is a common side effect, and it continued for five days. I called Dr. Rossi and together he and I decided to give Keppra a try. The neurologist who had diagnosed temporal lobe epilepsy had originally wanted to put me on this drug but had decided against it because of the increased possibility of anxiety as a side effect. I started off on a very small dosage of 250 milligrams. The good thing about Keppra, unlike the other two drugs I had tried, was that it took effect immediately. After a week, I had no side effects other than a tired feeling, which I eventually got used to with time.

Another EEG was ordered where twenty-four wires were glued to my scalp. After spending the night in the hospital, the EEG wires were finally removed the next day. It took a great deal of time because they had to rub acetone into my head. Then I was sent down for another MRI. Unlike my first MRI, this was a closed MRI. I feared being in closed spaces. It brought on panic attacks because they reminded me of being held down and unable to escape during my abuse. I get claustrophobic very easily.

I closed my eyes as I was backed into the closed machine. At the very end of the procedure, I was pulled out then pushed back in for the final part of the MRI. I decided I was strong enough to face my fears and opened my eyes, at which point I discovered that I had nothing to fear. No panic set in. Instead, I stayed calm and relaxed. Once finished, it was time to go home.

A half hour after returning home, I received a call from Dr. Rossi. He had looked at the EEG and MRI. He said the EEG showed a couple of extra-large spikes and the MRI clearly showed the problem. He described the cluster of scar cells near my temporal lobe that he determined I have had since birth. These scar cells are called astrocytes. They can irritate the surrounding normal brain cells. He explained that because I have had them my whole life and experienced my first seizure at twenty-three, it was possible that I could go the rest of my life without ever having another one.

Dr. Rossi explained that the medication Keppra keeps this localized irritation from spreading throughout the other brain pathways. Because there was activity on the EEG, he told me he would like me to stay on Keppra for two years and, if everything looked clear in the next EEG at that time, he would try taking me off it. He explained that the scar cells that formed had clearly blocked the area that controlled my sense of smell. After so many years of never understanding why I could not smell anything, it all made sense. I was glad I had gotten a second opinion.

After months of being unable to drive and having to rely on family members to take me to and from my internship, and even having coworkers drive me home (which I was grateful for since I worked until midnight), Dr. Rossi sent me paperwork saying I was safe to drive. It had been nearly four months since I had the seizure. Even with his approval, it took me several months to feel comfortable driving again. Because I had the seizure while driving, I had horrible anxiety every time I got into my car. I feared I would have another one. However, I couldn't spend my life letting fear control me. I had to learn to stop worrying and remind myself that I had God's protection.

Life changed a lot for me that year. We can look at the events that happen in our lives and come to many conclusions. I was not going to let fear control me. As with everything else, I would come to a place of acceptance, and I would learn to adjust. A pity party would get me nowhere. I could sit around feeling sorry for myself over the many obstacles I have faced, but what would this do for me? I could spend my life throwing my hands up in the air saying, "Why is this happening to me? What did I do to deserve this?" But what I have learned in the past is that you may never get the answers you seek, and you will just stay depressed.

Instead, I had to learn to start to accept the hand I was dealt, the same way I had learned to accept the vision problems, sexual abuse, and learning disability. I had to accept all of my obstacles, get up every day, and focus on the things that were important in my life. First and foremost, I am an author and an activist. While I was distracted for a period of time with these unforeseen challenges, I had to get back up and keep going. I needed to celebrate the huge accomplishments I had worked so hard to achieve, one of which was finally here, just months after my seizure—an accomplishment several people doubted I would ever achieve.

On May 10, 2008, four years after graduating high school, I graduated with honors from Western Illinois University with my degree in social work. This achievement was not about proving the people who doubted me wrong or making my parents proud, but rather about accomplishing a goal I had cherished since elementary school. I was following my dreams.

I jumped into my master's program in July immediately after graduating college. For the school year 2008–2009, I worked in a high school three days a week as a school social work intern. I had a caseload of students with and without learning disabilities. Little did the students with learning disabilities know, I could relate. I was attending some of the very same meetings I used to sit in as a student in high school. The difference now was that I wasn't the student. Instead, I was the one providing the information I gathered during assessments and conducting social histories. I would give student, parent, and teacher rating scales called the Behavior Assessment System for Children, second edition (BASC-2). After gathering all this information, I put the responses into our system and it provided detailed information on the student that I would share at the student's conference.

I especially remember one freshman student who I worked with sitting in front of me in my office in tears saying how he felt stupid because he had a learning disability. I did everything I could to tell him he was not stupid and that he shouldn't let his learning disability stop him from his dreams. "If anything, let it be your determination to prove that it won't stop you," I told him. "Everyone has challenges they face, and they should not allow their challenges or obstacles to stop them from accomplishing their goals." He was unaware that I, too, had a learning disability. It is unethical to share personal information, so I was unable to disclose this to him.

Just as quickly as the school year started, it was ending. I was saying good-bye to the students I worked with all year, hoping something that I said along the way would stay with them as they continued on their life journeys.

Grad school was a lot more work than undergrad. I spent an entire year dedicated to school and school only. Most weekends were spent writing papers or studying. I did very well in grad school. On May 10, 2009, a year to the day after graduating with my bachelor's in social work, I walked up and accepted my diploma for my master's degree. It was a beautiful ceremony outside on the campus lawn of Aurora University. The sky was blue and the sun was shining bright as a bagpiper led us out of the ceremony.

Five years after graduating from high school, I had earned my master's degree. I remember looking up to the sky and thanking God. He gave me the strength to see that I had it in me all along to accomplish this. I had this driving force steering me in the right direction, never wavering no matter what obstacles fell upon my path.

My sister and I in the room we were interviewed in as kids, in the Children's Advocacy Center, the day Erin's Law was signed in Illinois.

Illinois Representative Jerry Mitchell and Senator Tim Bivins, both sponsors of Erin's Law.

©POWELL PHOTOGRAPHY, INC.

Governor Quinn signing Erin's Law, January 24, 2013. Illinois was the first state to pass it.

My sister and I standing with Governor Quinn the day Erin's Law was signed.

POWELL PHOTOGRAPHY, INC.

©Lou Rocco/Disney-ABC Domestic Television.

Katie Couric interviewing me on her show in March 2013.

©Lou Rocco/Disney-ABC Domestic Television.

Standing with Katie Couric after being a guest on her show discussing Erin's Law.

©Harpo Productions, Inc./All Rights Reserved/Photographer: George Burns

Standing with Oprah Winfrey after being interviewed on her show in October 2010.

Interview on WWMT News in Kalmazoo, Michigan, with Senator John Proos and newscaster Josh Roe, July 2012.

All smiles in Arkansas with Representative John Baine, just after testifying and Erin's Law passing, March 2013. Arkansas was the seventh state to pass it.

Testifying at the capitol to Pennsylvania legislators in September 2012.

Testifying at capitol in Michigan in July 2012 with sponsor Senator John Proos.

Standing with Senator John Proos and Michigan Governor Rick Snyder. Michigan was the fifth state to pass Erin's Law.

Receiving a round of applause, standing on stage in Carnegie Hall for Glamour's Women of the Year Awards, November 2012.

Actress Julianna Margulies with my sister and me during Glamour's Women of the Year Awards.

Seated with Rory, Ethel and Kerry Kennedy at dinner after Glamour's Women of the Year Awards. Ethel and Rory Kennedy were also honored as women of the year.

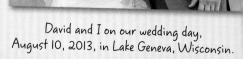

David and I on our wedding day, August 10, 2013, in Lake Geneva, Wisconsin.

Erin's Law

**THE JOURNEY OF
A THOUSAND MILES BEGINS
WITH ONE STEP.**

—Lao-tzu

Six months after graduating with my master's in social work, my second book, entitled *Living for Today*, was published. In it, I finally opened up about being raped as a young child and my battle with anorexia during my four years of college. Dropping down to ninety-two pounds my senior year, my eating disorder gave me the control that was taken from me at the precious age of six. The man who raped me avoided authorities even as they tried to track him down in 2007. He wasn't denying it. He just wasn't talking. Eventually pleading the fifth, the detectives' hands were tied, and there was no more they could do without physical evidence.

While I may never see him behind bars in this life, I know I will eventually get justice. I am glad that after sixteen years of staying silent, he knew that I was the one who turned him in and that I was no longer afraid. I wish I had found my voice at a much earlier age. However, nobody ever taught me to speak up and not keep these secrets, so I stayed silent.

I began my new job working as a youth and family counselor at a counseling agency five months after graduation. I eventually had a large caseload of families. I was running substance abuse groups, a girls' after-school program, groups in one of the local middle schools, and a program in the same high school I did my internship at. I did a lot of family counseling, working with parents and youth, mostly in the evening. I loved helping families build healthier relationships and deal with challenging situations. I loved to see the growth they made several months after meeting them.

I was also on call for crisis calls that came in. I eventually got labeled by a coworker of mine as "the crisis chick." Anytime I was on crisis, the phone started ringing. During my first month on the job,

I was trained in doing suicidal and homicidal assessments on youth. I would use both skills during my time working there. I sent several youth that I determined were a threat to themselves, and others, to the hospital. I dealt with crisis calls that involved runaway teens, parents discovering drugs in their youth's room, even a situation where I was called to the police department to handle a domestic violence situation between a teen and his mother.

Five months into my job, God spoke to me one night to do something else that had been weighing heavily on my heart for years. I had a vision to get a law passed that would mandate that children be taught sexual-abuse education in schools. A year earlier, I reached out to my local senator on the subject. He agreed we should educate children on this, but he told me that I was talking about a taboo topic, and that I would never get it passed. He told me that people would vote against it, believing that this topic should be left to be taught in the home. I told him about the number of children abused at home by their parents, relatives, or caretakers each year, and how many parents fear this topic so they avoid talking about it or naively think it would never happen to their child. I told him that if he would not help me, I would find a legislator who would. I was ready to end the taboo and stigma surrounding sexual abuse by educating society, especially children.

I constantly felt God nudging me to not doubt myself on this decision. I knew my full-time job as a youth and family counselor would not allow the time for what I felt I was called to do. I knew that if I had a goal I wanted to accomplish, I could get it done. While I thought my calling was to help survivors of abuse find their voices, I soon discovered in the spring of 2010 that I had a much bigger purpose— a purpose to get a law passed to protect and educate children from abuse. I was hearing God say to me, "Quit your job and go after this law. I will provide. You will accomplish this mission. Trust me. You will have doubters, but you will accomplish this." While God continued to put this on my heart, I was struggling with the idea of trying to explain to my parents that I was going to resign from my job to go after getting a law passed because God told me to.

In March 2010, after putting a lot of thought and prayer into it, and God putting it on my heart every night as I lay in bed, I met with my boss and handed him my letter of resignation. I agreed to work until April 30 to help during the center's busiest time of year. He handed my letter back to me and asked me to think about this more over the weekend. He asked what he could change for me at work so I would stay. I explained to him that I was not leaving the agency to work at another job, but, instead, I was leaving on a mission my heart was dedicated to that would be very time-consuming, and that my job at the counseling agency just wouldn't allow me to fulfill it. I used all my vacation days throughout April for speaking engagements. It is the busiest time of year for me when it comes to travel, since April is Child Abuse Prevention Month. On April 30, I worked my last day, feeling confident in this mission I was heading toward. I found my voice on April 30, 1998; I confronted my cousin on April 30, 2003; and now I resigned from my job on April 30, 2010, to strive for my purpose in life.

Many people might think that I was out of my mind for resigning from my job in order to fight for a law on a taboo topic. Resigning meant no paycheck during a time when many were desperate for employment after being laid off during a tough economy—and here I was, just walking away from mine. While my mission would not bring in any income, I was dedicated to it and determined to see change. It didn't matter what others thought. I didn't care if people thought I was nuts. I stopped caring what others thought of me in high school.

I knew in my heart that if I truly believed, I could achieve whatever I wanted to accomplish. I would get it done. One thing I knew for sure was that I was being led by God and to listen when he had my attention. I am always confident in the direction he leads me.

In January 2010, I wrote every senator in the state of Illinois about my vision for Erin's Law and the importance of educating kids on sexual abuse in school. The following month, I spoke at a child abuse conference in the small town of Dixon, Illinois, the boyhood hometown of President Ronald Reagan. I shared with the audience my mission to get Erin's Law passed, thus empowering kids to use their voices and tell someone if something inappropriate ever happened. I told the crowd that as a child, it was required (and still is now) that schools do tornado drills, bus drills, and fire drills. Then I pulled out a small black card I had received in sixth grade. It was my DARE card. I told the audience how DARE taught us how to say no to drugs and that the back of the card gives you the eight ways to say no. I looked at the audience and said, "Where were the eight ways on how to get away and how to tell today? They never came. So when I was raped and molested as a child, I listened to the only message I was given, and that was from the men abusing me, telling me to stay silent."

I read an entry from my childhood diary to the audience that I wrote when I was twelve years old. This is what it said:

May 1997

I sobbed the whole way home. A guy called Officer Friendly comes to school and teaches us not to answer the door when your parents are not home and don't talk to strangers. They don't teach us about people like my cousin Brian. I thought people like Brian jumped out of bushes and attacked you at night. They never warned us in school about our own family. I am so afraid. God protect me.

Had someone been educating me about safe touch and unsafe touch, I honestly believe I would have had the strength to tell immediately instead of waiting years to come forward. Unfortunately, we don't teach kids in school about sexual abuse. We make sure to include lesson plans on what kids should do if they are being pushed around on the playground or what to do when a stranger on the Internet asks to meet up with them, but nothing that empowers them to tell if someone sexually abuses them.

According to the U.S. Department of Justice, 93 percent of children know their abuser. That means that 7 percent of the time, the abuser is a stranger. Yet we focus so much on stranger danger with children. Parents are more concerned about someone snatching their child at the bus stop than they are about something happening during a family gathering or during their after-school activities, sports, or sleepovers. I am determined to get Erin's Law passed to educate kids in school. I do not want to fail the next generation of children. I set out to see my vision of Erin's Law passed in my state of Illinois. I trusted myself and banished all self-doubt from my mind. In my heart I knew I could do this.

After finishing my speech in Dixon, Illinois, I was immediately approached by Dan Langloss, the chief of police. He told me that he wanted to help me with my mission with Erin's Law, and that he wanted to introduce me to Tim Bivins, the local senator in Dixon, to see if he could help us.

A month later, I was back in Dixon, Illinois, joining the chief at Senator Bivins's office to discuss Erin's Law. I sat before Senator Bivins, briefly sharing my background, my mission, and what I wanted this law to address. I included why it is so important to teach kids about sexual abuse. I also informed him of my recent resignation from my job to get this law passed. Senator Bivins heard my passion and agreed to help me. He explained that he would draft a bill and see what he could get accomplished before the Senate recessed for the summer. He asked if I would be willing to testify on the bill before the Senate. I told him I would do whatever it took to get this law heard and passed. On April 29, 2010, Senator Bivins submitted Senate Bill 2843 (SB2843), also known as Erin's Law.

This law created a task force that would make recommendations for reducing child sexual abuse in Illinois. The task force had to submit its final report to the governor with its recommendations. The law allowed schools to adopt and implement a policy addressing sexual abuse of children to include age-appropriate curriculum for students in pre-K through fifth grade, training for school personnel on child sexual abuse, and educational information for parents or guardians to be provided in the school handbook on the warning signs of a child being abused, along with contact information for anyone needing assistance, a referral list, and additional resources.

I was informed that we could not go after the mandated bill just yet, as an unfunded mandate would never get passed. We first had to do our research on existing curriculum, the process schools must go through to implement this curriculum, how often, and the training behind it. The first week of May 2010 was the final week before the Senate and the House would recess for the summer. It was a long shot, but I was praying Erin's Law would be heard. Senator Bivins informed me that we may not know until the day before. Since I had just resigned from my job, I had the flexibility. I just needed enough notice to make the three-and-a-half-hour drive to the state capital. I got a call just before 8:00 PM from Senator Bivins informing me that the bill had been called to be heard in the Senate the next morning at 9:00 AM. This called for an early morning of getting up at 3:00 AM to make the three-hour trip to the capital of Illinois to testify before the Senate Education Committee.

When Chief Langloss and I arrived at the capitol, we met with Senator Bivins in his office and discussed how I would testify. He told me to keep it to ten minutes, otherwise I would either be cut off or lose the senators' attention. He also encouraged me not to get angry. He had seen other people who had been victimized get angry while testifying on bills, and it was not beneficial. I told him he had nothing to worry about. That would not happen. Senator Bivins, a Republican, informed me that Democrats were the majority, and while we would have the Republican vote, my job was to convince the Democrats. I told him I would give it my all.

I sat at a table with dozens of people behind me and thirteen senators sitting before me as Senator Bivins introduced me as a survivor, author, and nationally recognized speaker who had appeared on numerous talk shows. Then it was my turn to speak.

I glanced at each and every one of them as I began to testify:

As a child, I grew up in Illinois public schools where I got a great education. It was there that I was taught about fire drills, tornado drills, bus drills, stranger danger, and DARE in sixth grade. If you completed DARE, you got this card (I lifted up my sixth-grade DARE card). The card meant you completed the DARE program and agreed to say no to drugs. On the back of this card are the eight ways to say no to drugs. Where were the eight ways of how to get away and how to tell today when someone is sexually abusing you? They never came, and when I was just weeks shy of my seventh birthday, I sat in the bedroom of my best friend's house playing when her uncle walked into the room and locked the door. This man went on to lift me up on the bed and rape me. He told me not to tell anyone, or he would come and get me. Five years later, someone even closer in my life abused me; this time it was a teenaged cousin who molested me from age eleven to thirteen; he also warned me that no one would believe me if I told, and that this was our secret.

Sexual abuse is a silent epidemic in our society. I was taught about stranger danger, not to go look for that lost puppy or take candy. Yet the men who raped and abused me were not strangers, and more than 90 percent of the time when a child is abused, it is someone the child knows and the parents trust. Parents warn their kids about stranger danger and fear their children being snatched from the bus stop, when a majority of the time, children are being hurt by the people we love and trust.

I didn't have to run out of a burning building as a child. I never had to take cover from a tornado, and it was not a stranger who killed my innocence. If someone would have talked in school about safe touch and unsafe touch, I believe I would have spoken up as a child and not been victimized over and over again for years, but that day never came, which is why my mission now is to protect children from the childhood I could not be protected from. I fly all over the country speaking out on this epidemic, and each time I speak in a classroom at a high school or college, I ask the students how many remember stranger danger, DARE, and all the drills in elementary school. Every single hand goes up. Yet when I ask how many remember someone teaching them in school about safe touch and unsafe touch, safe secrets and unsafe secrets, how to get away and who to tell today, not a single hand in all these years has ever gone up. No matter where I am speaking, every time after I speak, someone comes up and breaks their silence, whether it is a student, an adult man, or a woman. Erin's Law will give students the tools and knowledge to speak up if someone ever tries to touch them or has already done so. I don't want children to keep the secrets I carried for years. My innocence was stolen and my trust was taken, but I have reclaimed my voice and want to educate and empower children with their voice. Now it's your time to give children a voice. Do it for the kids. Thank you all for your time; I truly appreciate it.

It was so quiet in that room when I spoke that you could hear a pin drop, and, when I finished, they all applauded. After the applause stopped, the committee chairperson, Democrat Senator Meeks, spoke into the microphone, "I will do anything you want!" Senator Bivins whispered in my ear, "Well, there are several bills of mine you can tell him to vote yes on." We both laughed.

Then a woman on the committee stood up and looked at me and said, "Erin, thank you so much for your courage and strength on speaking out on this. You are right. This is an epidemic and children need to be educated on this." She then turned to face the committee and said, "I want you all to hear what Erin has just said and vote in support of this bill." I was so pleased with how it was going.

Chief Langloss then testified about what he had seen in his job working with sexual abuse cases and the statistics about sexual abuse. Moments later, they all voted: thirteen yes and zero no. With everyone voting in support of Erin's Law, we were off to a great start. We walked outside the room, and moments later Senator Bivins shared with us that he had never seen someone get applause after testifying and could not believe that Senator Meeks had just told me he would do anything I wanted. Senator Bivins looked at me and said, "You nailed that with your testimony and could not have said it better. You wrapped it up perfect and got the point across, and the timing was great. You had all of their attention." He pointed out that I got all the feedback from the ones I needed to convince, the Democrats.

As we talked about our first accomplishment of the day, a woman who had just heard me testify came walking up to me and Senator Bivins. "Erin, I just want to say thank you so much for what you just did in there and what you are doing." Tears filled her eyes and began to stream down her face. "I was sexually abused as a child and am so happy someone is doing something about it by giving us a voice."

Senator Bivins stood there in complete silence. After exchanging some comforting words with this woman, Senator Bivins looked at me. "You were right. Someone does approach you after you speak and share their story. Wow!"

After he disclosed to a few other senators our previous discussion on the topic, I turned to him and said, "I've been doing this long enough to know what to expect."

We went back to Senator Bivins's office where we talked about what would happen next. The bill would be taken to the Senate floor to be voted on. Once voted on and approved by the Senate, it would go to the House, where I would testify just like I did that morning. If it passed in the House, it would be sent to the governor to be signed. So the waiting began, and it ended up turning into an extremely long day—one that began by getting up at 3:00 AM and ended with me not getting home until nearly midnight.

I watched as one bill after another was discussed and eventually voted on. Some bills took minutes for a vote, but others took anywhere between twenty to forty-five minutes as the two groups battled it out. This went on for hours, and we began to realize that the longer they spent talking, the smaller our chance was of getting Erin's Law heard and passed by the Senate that day and then on to the House to be voted on. During the day, a member of the House picked up the bill to sponsor the law, which was great. I walked onto the Senate floor with some senators. I spoke with many different senators through-out this very long day at the capitol, many telling me what powerful testimony I gave.

After hearing them vote on bills all day, they were down to their final four. In my opinion, they saved the best for last, SB2843, Erin's Law. Senator Bivins addressed the senators on the Senate floor at 6:00 PM. The voting began, and I watched the two huge screens light up.

Fifty-five yes and zero no. SB2843 passed without a single no vote all day. I was thrilled, knowing this would look excellent when it made its way to the House of Representatives to be voted on.

Because it was the last day in the session, Erin's Law would not be heard by the House until veto session in November. It was amazing how fast things moved. I had just met Senator Bivins three weeks earlier and told him about the law I envisioned for the children of our state. My childhood could not be saved, but I knew I had the power to do something positive by protecting future generations of children. I was looking ahead to one day when this law would be signed by our governor and children would be getting the education I never received.

As I drove home later that night after a long day at the capitol, I knew that there were children going to bed in that moment with the same secrets I carried as a child, children who feel so scared, confused, and alone in their pain that they bury their faces in their pillows and weep, children who have silent voices not yet strong enough to tell anyone the secrets they keep. It is that thought that keeps me going. I am on a mission to put sex offenders out of business by empowering children with their voices, which should never be silenced.

Chapter 15

Panic Attacks

So do not fear,
for I am with you;
do not be dismayed,
for I am your God.
I will strengthen you and
help you; I will uphold
you with my righteous
right hand.

—*Isaiah 41:10*

I had a lot going on in 2010. I resigned from my job, traveled across the country for speaking engagements, and pursued a law in Illinois. It had been two years since my seizure, and my hope was to get off my medication since I hadn't had any additional problems. I had every reason to be optimistic, as this was what my doctor had originally discussed with me. The results of my EEG recording of my brain told the same story it had two years prior. I had spiking and firing going on, and without medication I would still be at risk for more seizures. Surely, this was not the news I wanted to hear, but I had to accept it.

Dr. Rossi sent me to get a closed MRI of my brain at the hospital that May. Since I had done this before, I knew I would be fine. I had my fear of tight spaces under control. Once Dr. Rossi got the results of my MRI, he sent them to a top Alzheimer's specialist who was going to examine my brain further.

Shortly after these tests, I began having extremely bad auras. These are small seizures in which you don't lose consciousness, but everything seems to be going in slow motion and you become extremely light-headed. I also felt this awful tingling sensation shoot down the entire right side of my body. The sensation started in my head and shot down to my feet. It was one of the worst feelings, and I had an overwhelming sense of helplessness because I couldn't stop it. My only option was to lay down in case it turned into a tonic-clonic seizure. This would prevent the possibility of severe injury. Each time I had an aura, I called my doctor.

To me, the best way to describe an aura is to think about a time when you got up too fast and felt light-headed, like you were going to faint. Now multiply this by ten. Add to it a tingling sensation shooting down the side of your body with the world appearing to go into slow motion. Have you ever played a movie at a very slow speed, unable to make out what the people in the video were saying because the words were coming out too slow? This is how everything appears to me during an aura.

For the first two years, I had no problems and was on a small dose of 500 mgs of Keppra. However, later, when the auras began, my doctor increased my medication after each instance. The auras became stronger, and, after they passed, I began having panic attacks. Trembling and clammy, I would turn ghost white in a total state of panic that I just could not stop. Luckily, I was living with my parents at the time and had their support. They always came to my assistance each time it happened. I often isolated myself emotionally from my parents. I never wanted them to see my pain from the abuse I had endured growing up. At this time in my life, however, I could not isolate myself. The panic attacks were so extreme I would hold on to them, begging them to make it stop and to not leave my side. Anyone who has experienced this knows exactly what I mean.

In June 2010, I had just returned home from speaking to hundreds at a national conference in Washington, DC, about my mission with Erin's Law when I had another extremely bad aura that was followed by a terrifying panic attack. Once again, I was trembling and in a state of panic, breathing heavily with my heart racing. You could almost see my pulse ready to burst out of my skin. My mom suggested I take a hot bath, which she thought might calm my nerves.

"Why is this happening to me?" I asked, as tears streamed down my face.

"I wish I knew, Erin," she said.

No amount of words can describe the emotions going through me as my heart felt like it was ready to burst. I would have done anything to make it stop. Nobody could understand what I was experiencing. They were not living with my abnormal brain activity and the effects this had on me without warning. It was terrifying, and I felt trapped.

I began to believe that my auras may have sparked the panic attacks because they brought on a lot of the same feelings I felt as a child while being molested and raped, feelings of complete loss of control, fear, and confusion. While the aura would last anywhere from ten seconds to a minute, it always felt like an eternity for me, and I just wanted it to be over. Again, it was how I often felt as a child when being abused. Completely helpless and unable to make it stop, I knew I was vulnerable in those moments. Fear would take over, and as the sense of helplessness consumed me, my anxiety would increase. After the panic attacks were over, I would often cry in the darkness, much like I had as a child, but this time it was for different reasons.

My doctor made me come in and see him immediately after that aura in June 2010. Because he didn't want me driving, he had my mother bring me. We walked into Dr. Rossi's office and he asked if it would be okay if a medical student sat in on our conversation. I found this kind of strange but would later understand in our conversation why he wanted this medical student to sit in on what he was about to tell me.

My mother described these episodes of auras turning into panic attacks to my doctor.

"Her heart and pulse are racing, her body is clammy, and she turns white, and she won't let go of me. It is like she is a five-year-old again. The only way we have been able to calm her down is having her take a bath," she explained.

"You don't leave her in the bathtub alone?" Dr. Rossi asked. He feared me going into a full tonic-clonic seizure and drowning after these incidents.

My mother reassured him that she would never leave me alone. Dr. Rossi discussed increasing my medication and putting me on an antianxiety medication to take as needed whenever I had an aura, to hopefully prevent the panic attacks.

"Now, I want to talk to you about the MRI you had last month. I sent your MRI to a neurologist that is a specialist with the brain who examined it up close and even sliced apart each section of the brain. A portion of the left temporal lobe of your brain is gone as the result of a case of viral encephalitis eating away at it as an infant," he explained.

"Wait! Did you just say a portion of my brain is gone?" I asked.

My mom's mouth dropped as she looked at me. We were both sitting there speechless. A million thoughts were running through my mind at that moment. He described how babies are resilient. That I was resilient as an infant and that the area of my brain where speech, writing, and short-term memory is stored is gone. He explained that my brain must've rewired itself to the right side in order for me learn how to do the things normally controlled by the left side of my brain.

To help me visualize this, he explained that a portion the size of a medium potato was missing from the left temporal lobe of my brain. Imagine for a minute a doctor telling you this. It didn't make sense to me that this was just being revealed to me. How did my doctors not see this in MRIs before? Let me tell you that it is a very reassuring thought given all my struggles. It suddenly made sense now. The brain damage caused by this affected my short-term memory, the part of the brain used to retain information, the area where I struggled to retain so much information academically. Like I had always explained, I could do a math equation with an example in front of me, but my mind went blank without it, and I could only remember the first step or two. I know my learning disability was all linked to this. Shockingly, brain damage couldn't even stop me from pursuing what I set out to accomplish in life.

He said that the success I have had in life with this was truly amazing, and, if I got encephalitic as an adult, I would have a list of complications, including speech and memory. He told me that it would be very noticeable that something was wrong if this happened to me as an adult. Because it happened as an infant, however, my brain was able to rewire itself and I was able to learn how to speak and write. I believe that because of my academic struggles, the short-term memory never completely rewired itself to the right side. I honestly believe that because of my weak short-term memory, my long-term memory is that much stronger.

Dr. Rossi said that the miracle of it all was not just the fact that I didn't have any speech or writing difficulties, but that I am gifted in the area of speech, and that I went on to be a published author before even graduating high school. He stated that I needed to be written about in medical journals. At that, he glanced at the medical student in the room, who seemed to be taking it all in.

"Of course, we would keep your identity anonymous," he said.

I knew this was something incredibly unique and that I would have no problem sharing with others. It was just one more piece of the puzzle that I was beginning to put together. It was all so surreal to hear.

My mother told him about my ability to remember facts and dates of things that happened over a decade or more ago and how I could give a play-by-play of any insignificant event. Unfortunately, I could also recount very painful details of ones that I wished I could forget.

Missing a part of my brain was certainly shocking news to hear, but it answered so many questions. I remember writing in my diary as a kid wondering if there was something wrong with my brain. Well, there certainly was. The portion of my brain that was eaten away by viral encephalitis left scar tissue, and it was the scar tissue that was irritating my brain and causing the spiking, firing, and auras that could eventually lead to a tonic-clonic seizure.

We left the doctor's office that day with news you would never expect nor want to hear, an increase in my medication, and a prescription for antianxiety medication to take in the event I had any more panic attacks. I asked Dr. Rossi why I was suddenly having all these auras after two years of being problem free. He explained that this was common in many patients. He called it the two-year honeymoon stage, which ultimately ended once my brain adjusted to the medication and it could no longer protect me at that dosage. That was why he increased it and discussed the possibility of having to look into another drug if the auras continued. For two years, I had been looking forward to the idea of not having to take medication, and now I was willing to take anything just to make these horrible auras and panic attacks stop.

We don't know what each day will bring us, but I have learned to appreciate each day for what it is and to be grateful for the life I have been given. Even through all the pain, confusion, frustration, and heartache, it has continued to make me a stronger person. I have learned to keep moving forward with determination, courage, and faith. Sometimes in life, we take the little things for granted. I wake up every morning and the first thing I do before getting out of bed is thank God for this day, whatever it may bring. I know he is right there with a helping hand in everything I am doing.

Chapter 16

Interview of a Lifetime

**TURN YOUR WOUNDS
INTO WISDOM.**

—*Oprah Winfrey*

One afternoon on August 2, 2010, as I sat at a coffee shop in Wisconsin, completely focused on writing, with my fingers tapping the keyboard of my laptop, I realized I had not written to *The Oprah Winfrey Show* in quite a long time. I knew that after twenty-five years, they were about to begin taping Oprah's final season. I checked out her "Be on the Show" page on her website. Sure enough, there was a story topic called "Were you sexually abused as a child?" I wrote a brief message about being abused and my movement with Erin's Law. After clicking "send," I went back to my writing and didn't think much more about it since I had written so many times in the past. The furthest I got in the process was an invitation to come to a few tapings, but I never got to share my personal journey and message.

I returned the next day to the local coffee shop. I was sipping my coffee and writing the beginning stages of this book when a phone call distracted me. I looked down to see a number I recognized. I knew immediately it was Harpo Studios. That is what happens when you have received so many calls from them. They were calling in response to the message I had sent on Oprah's website about being a survivor of sexual abuse. For the next hour, I sat on the phone with a producer who asked me questions about my own experience with sexual abuse, forgiveness, and what I have taken away from Oprah's show over the years—a platform that she has used to discuss her own personal experience as a survivor and where other survivors have shared their stories. By now, my answers were routine since I had spoken to so many producers in the past, yet nothing ever came of it. My reasoning for contacting the show in the past was because I wanted nothing more than to simply put a face and voice on sexual abuse. But now, my mission was to talk about Erin's Law. I continued to write in because I was confident that my day to tell my story would eventually come.

The producer who I had just spoken to for more than an hour told me she would call me back the next day. While I was not going to get my hopes up, I knew this would be my last chance and it would be perfect timing since I was on a mission to get a law passed that would educate and protect kids.

Oprah made it acceptable for survivors everywhere not to be silenced or ashamed. I remember thinking I would never get to that place. I thought only Oprah could get there because of who she was. As I got older, I would come to learn differently. No amount of fame or money can bring happiness and peace. You have to discover that on your own and strive for it.

The producer called asking for the letter my cousin sent to me apologizing. She mentioned that they were looking at having me read the letter and share what his apology did for me. I loved the sound of it all, but I really wanted to know if I could talk about how forgiveness led me to do something positive in my life by going after Erin's Law. It was forgiving my cousin that sent me on this crusade in the first place. So much freedom came from that. But producers kept telling me that they didn't know if I would be able to talk about Erin's Law.

I still didn't want to believe that this was really going to happen after more than a decade of trying to appear on Oprah's show. It really began to hit me when on August 25, the producer I had been talking to and a camera crew showed up at my home at 10:00 AM to begin setting up equipment to interview me. I was used to this by now from my other experiences of appearing on *Good Morning America, The Montel Williams Show*, and local media interviews on how they might ask me a question, and then I would just look into the camera and speak from my heart. The producer felt very confident in me and told me to share my story and explain how Oprah's show impacted me on my own journey to healing.

As I looked into the camera, I knew the words I shared would be heard by millions. I couldn't mess up. This was what I worked so hard to achieve since I was thirteen years old after finding my voice for the first time. Eleven years of waiting for this moment and it was finally here. I didn't give up, and I knew that when the time was right, it would happen, and it came down to the very end in her final season. We finished taping the interview, which I had poured my heart into, by 4:00 PM.

The morning that I had worked so hard to get to had finally arrived. It was September 2, 2010, and at 6:30 AM, a car had arrived to take my sister and me to Harpo Studios. I was so happy that morning as we made our way to downtown Chicago. So many emotions were running through me. It was a gloomy, cloudy, and rainy day, but that didn't matter, because I knew I was about to put a bright light on a very dark, taboo topic, and millions would hear this message.

Once we arrived, my sister and I were checked in by security and then taken upstairs to the green room. My sister was enjoying all the yummy treats that were provided. She was just enjoying the moment. She wasn't the one about to speak on national television with Oprah and the world watching.

It was so surreal. I was about to be talking with Oprah and to the largest audience I would likely ever have. I was eventually greeted by a man from a legal team and asked to sign some legal documents. I was then hooked up to a microphone and a makeup artist came to do my makeup. As we were taken downstairs, we passed by many poster-size photos of Oprah over the years with the guests and celebrities she had interviewed. I was brought into another green room where the producer I had been working with was talking to another guest who was to appear on the show. She was going over what Oprah would be discussing with the guest. We were eventually told that the show was about to begin, but the producer still had not discussed with me what questions to expect from Oprah. The producer glanced at me behind stage just before going out to the studio and said, "I am not worried about you at all. You got this. You are a great speaker."

I was told just moments before taking my seat in the front row of the audience that I could talk about Erin's Law, but to keep it brief and to the point, so it wouldn't be edited out, which would happen if I talked about it for too long. I wanted to jump for joy when I heard the news. This law had turned into my life mission, and to be able to share it with a viewing audience as large as Oprah's was going to be amazing.

I sat front row in a reserved seat along with the rest of the guests for the show. My sister sat a row behind me. The show began with a mother from London who had dissociative identity disorder and her daughter. Then it focused on Truddi, a previous guest of Oprah's who had since passed away. Her daughter Kari was there to talk about growing up with a mother with dissociative identity disorder and how the sexual abuse her mother had suffered also impacted both their lives.

Then it went to my interview I had done from home. A day of taping was edited down to two minutes and thirteen seconds, which had me sharing what had happened to me in my childhood. Photos and home videos of me as a young child played across the screen. I shared with Oprah how thankful I was to her and Truddi for being so brave to speak openly and honestly about their abuse on national television and that it made me realize I was not alone in my suffering. Immediately after my segment aired, Oprah spoke.

"Wow, that is really powerful. Thank you for that. Really, I am so moved by that." Tears began to stream down Oprah's face. Oprah looked at Truddi's daughter Kari and said, "Your mom's life made a difference," and then she looked out to the audience and said, "When you do these shows, you just never know who is watching and who will break their own silence." Those same tears I saw in the television show from Oprah talking about her abuse so many years earlier I saw in person that September day in the studio once again before an audience of millions.

With tears streaming down her face, Oprah went to commercial. During the break, Oprah looked to the audience. "Now that Erin has me crying and all of you crying, I need my makeup team out here."

I really did not expect the reaction I got from Oprah. She kept looking over at me and smiling during commercial breaks after that. After speaking for some time with Truddi Chase's daughter Kari, there came the point in the show I had been waiting for. Oprah would call it "Erin's Call for Action." After Oprah came back from a commercial break, she turned to me.

"Erin, I want to talk to you for a moment. I understand you demanded an apology from your abuser?"

I described to Oprah how, after going down a destructive path, I wanted to let go of the anger and hatred and move forward, and to be able to forgive. After seven months of e-mail correspondence with this family member, I finally got the apology I was looking for.

Oprah then asked, "Did he acknowledge having abused you?"

"Yes, he did very openly share what he did and admitted he was wrong, and if you'd like, I can share a piece of what he wrote in his letter."

"Yes, tell me what he said."

I then read off a card that already had his apology letter printed on it. After reading the letter, I looked at Oprah and said, "And it was this letter that finally allowed me to come out of darkness and decide I want to put a face and voice on this silent epidemic, because like

Truddi and millions of others who have suffered through this horror, we don't talk about this in our society. We are shunned, people
are stigmatized, there is shame attached to this, and we don't educate
children about this. We teach kids tornado drills, fire drills, bus drills.
We put all this information into their heads but teach them nothing
about sexual abuse, and that is why I went after a law in the State of
Illinois called Erin's Law, which was recently passed by the Senate. It
is a law that will demand education."

I was about to explain the law when Oprah excitedly said "Good
for you!" The audience erupted in applause.

"And I plan to take this law national because kids need to be educated on sexual abuse. They need the tools to speak up," I said.

"I think kids need to be educated and I think parents need to be
educated," Oprah said.

"Yes, and that is also a part of it," I agreed.

"Thank you, thank you so much," Oprah replied.

When the show was over and the camera stopped rolling, Oprah
stood up onstage and walked directly in front of my seat. Looking
down at me, she told her audience, "Erin is an inspiration to me in the
work I have done on this issue for the past twenty-five years."

Before leaving that day, I stood onstage with Oprah and looked
into a camera, smiling as we took a photo together. It was a moment
in time I will never forget, a moment I knew would come because I
never gave up.

The show aired on October 6, 2010. Each hour it played across
America, my e-mail and Facebook page lit up with messages. Thousands of letters poured in from people sharing their stories, thanking
me for my courage, and telling me they would stand behind Erin's Law
and hoped to get it passed in their own states. It was incredible to see
so many people get on board. Many people over the twenty-five years

of *The Oprah Winfrey Show* wanted to get on her favorite things show or to sell a product to become wealthy. Her ability to make things happen was eventually termed the "Oprah Effect." I believe gifts and money do not buy happiness. Knowing children are being educated and empowered on sexual abuse prevention is what brings me overwhelming happiness. A year later, I was interviewed again on Oprah's new network OWN, and talked about forgiveness.

There was still work to do on Erin's law. It had only passed in the Senate and I still needed to testify to the House in Illinois and then get the governor's support of this law with his signature. I was set to testify to the House Education Committee on November 17, 2010. Just as I was coming off one of the greatest experiences of my life, things would take yet another drastic turn that I had not anticipated. It was as if I turned off the path I was on to come upon a dead end, and if I didn't find my way out, I feared I wouldn't survive.

Chapter 17

Roadblock

LIFE HAS KNOCKED ME
DOWN A FEW TIMES. IT SHOWED
ME THINGS I NEVER WANTED
TO SEE. I EXPERIENCED SADNESS
AND FAILURES. BUT ONE THING IS
FOR SURE, I ALWAYS GET UP!

—*Author unknown*

On Saturday, October 30, 2010, I went to a friend's Halloween party. It was a great night and I stayed out late. It was 1:30 AM by the time I arrived home. Minutes after I walked in the door, I heard the front door opening again. It was my sister coming home from her night out. We talked for a few minutes and said good night to each other. I climbed into bed and closed my eyes just after 2:00 AM. I didn't wake up to my very large cat, Bailey, nudging me like he does every morning. Nor did I wake to the light peering through my windows. It was still dark out when I woke up to my dad, mom, and sister standing around my bed. I was in a state of complete confusion and panic. I was so confused that they were in my room, and I felt like I was having a panic attack at the same time. They were all talking to me at once, making it hard to make out what was going on. I didn't feel right and had overwhelming anxiety.

"What is going on?" I asked them.

"Erin, you had a seizure," Mom cried.

The confusion and anxiety suddenly turned into a full-blown panic attack. I was holding on to my mother, trembling and crying. This was nothing new by now. They were accustomed to me having panic attacks, but this was the first time they witnessed me having a seizure, and my sister described it later as "scaring the daylights out of her."

"What? What do you mean I had a seizure?"

"Erin, five minutes after I went to my room, I heard this strange noise coming from your room. I first thought it was the cat throwing up. Then I jumped out of bed because it sounded like it was coming from you. I went into your room and your entire body was shaking and your eyes were rolled back in your head. I ran to get Mom and Dad out of bed."

"No, no don't tell me that," I said to her.

My dad was rubbing my back, saying it was going to be okay. I immediately grabbed my mother's hand and pulled her near me and then began sobbing. By now they knew only one way to calm me during a panic attack, and that was a hot bath.

The next morning I called my doctor and he upped my medication. By October 2010, my medication went from the smallest dosage of 500 mgs of Keppra for two years to suddenly, after each aura I had, 750 mgs, 1,000 mgs, 1,500 mgs, 1,750 mgs, and, a month earlier, 2,000 mgs. After the seizure, he raised it to 2,500 mgs, which was 2,000 mgs more than seven months earlier. For the longest time, I didn't want to be on medication; now I just didn't want to have more seizures, and I'd take anything to make them stop.

The day after my seizure, I woke to the same pain I felt the first time it happened. Every muscle in my body was sore. It felt like they were all pulled. The slightest movement hurt. No amount of ibuprofen helped. I didn't want to move, and the only way to do that was sleep.

A day after Dr. Rossi upped my medication by 500 mgs, I started to feel different. I didn't feel like myself. All the times in the past when my medication was raised, I felt no different, this time I felt like all the motivation I had was drained out of me. I thought that maybe because of the beating my body took from the seizure, my mind and body were just exhausted.

The driving force in me to accomplish anything I set my mind to seemed to disappear overnight. Each passing hour seemed to get worse. A few days after the seizure and my medication being increased, I found myself not even wanting to get out of bed, and it wasn't because my muscles were sore. They weren't that painful anymore. I didn't have any motivation or desire to shower or get dressed. I found myself just staying in my pajamas all day. I went from speaking passionately on

Erin's Law at a conference in Maryland two weeks earlier to finding it difficult to motivate myself to do simple tasks like showering, changing, and eating. I stopped answering my phone and responding to e-mails. The little things I never gave much thought to now became a challenge. All I wanted to do was sleep. It was freaking me out, and I just wanted to feel like myself again.

I went from feeling like I was on the world's tallest mountain ready to conquer anything I set my mind to, to suddenly feeling as if I was at the bottom of the Grand Canyon desperate to climb out. Overnight, it felt like someone had turned the light off inside me—a light I had spent years trying to turn on. I felt empty and depressed, with sudden dark thoughts of killing myself. When my thoughts started to turn to thinking about ways to end my life, I knew something was seriously wrong. I was getting intense suicidal thoughts while at the same time knowing suicide was completely wrong. I kept telling myself, *I am going out of my mind. I am not a suicidal person. I am the happiest person. Snap out of it.* It was terrifying me that I was thinking this way.

My family saw the change in me. They just didn't know how dark things had gotten. The dark thoughts only got worse, and I had never felt this hopeless in my entire life. I had thought of several ways to end my life and was ready to act on them. I knew I was not thinking clearly and something was seriously wrong with me. The war inside me was getting darker every passing minute.

I went from working in a youth and family counseling agency as a therapist doing suicidal assessments at my last job just six months earlier to suddenly being the one thinking this way. I tried with everything I had to snap out of it. There was this overwhelming sense of shame I felt about thinking this way. I knew this was not a healthy way of thinking, yet I couldn't turn these dangerously dark thoughts off.

I kept thinking I would shake it off and eventually wake up and feel like myself again. I was embarrassed. How could I go from a person pursuing all her goals to thinking about ending her life? I didn't want anyone to know I felt this way, so I just kept praying I would wake up and once again be ready to bring change to this world and conquer everything I set out to do.

I think the best thing that came out of getting my master's degree in social work was that it ended up saving my own life. All my training allowed me to have the intuitive knowledge that something was seriously wrong. I knew the medication I was on had something to do with my thought process after my doctor raised it. I could still think clearly enough to know that if I didn't do something soon, I might stop thinking and act on my suicidal thoughts. I knew I had only one option if I was going to live to see another day and continue on with my mission.

I continued to tell my parents that my medication was making me feel like I was going out of my mind, and, on the night of November 8, just nine days after I had the seizure, my older sister Caitlin called to talk to me. She began rambling on and on about how I needed to hand all this fear and confusion I was going through over to God. That God would take care of me. My mother was sitting in the dining room with me listening when I finally responded to my sister. "You have no idea what I am going through! You do not know what this medication has done to me. I can't think straight. I feel I am going out of my mind and just want myself back. I am sorry, but you don't understand, and I can't talk to you right now. Good-bye."

I handed the phone over to my mom, "I know you are just trying to help Erin, but we don't know what she is going through. Her medication is doing something to her; she hasn't been herself in a week. Keep praying for her."

Once off the phone with my sister, I looked at my mom and broke down and began sobbing. "A week ago I was happy and driven to get a law passed. Now I am ready to kill myself. I could walk out this door right now and have no problem jumping off a bridge. It would be so easy for me to do, and I would not think twice about it. I can't think clearly. Everything is so dark inside me. I am ready to die and go be with God."

A look of sheer panic came across my mother's face. "I would rather see you having a seizure right now than hear you talking like this."

"Mom, this isn't me. It is the drugs making me think this way. I need to get off them as soon as possible before I act on these crazy thoughts. You know this isn't me. I am sane enough to know this is wrong but insane enough to act on them." I had an oxymoron going on inside me.

"You call your doctor right now and tell him it is an emergency!" she cried.

At 9:30 PM, my mother stood next to me as I dialed my doctor's emergency number. He picked up and I told him how I was feeling the side effects of the drugs like depression, anxiety, emptiness, and no motivation. My mother was standing next to me.

"Tell him everything you told me," she demanded.

I feared telling him because I didn't want to end up in a mental hospital. I had to be very careful with my words. "Things are so dark. I am having suicidal thoughts," I said.

He immediately asked me to lower my medication by 500 mgs. "Do you plan on acting on these thoughts tonight?" he asked.

"No, I won't," I told him.

"Okay. I need you to make a safety plan with your mom. If you wake up in the middle of the night and feel you will act on these thoughts you are having, you will go wake up your mom," he said.

I could not believe I was making a safety plan to not kill myself.

"I am not going to act on these thoughts tonight, but, if that happens, I will wake my mom," I said.

"Get some sleep, and I will call you in the morning."

The next morning he called. "Are you still having suicidal thoughts?" he asked.

"The feelings are all still there," I explained.

"Is anyone home with you?" he asked.

"No, everyone is working," I told him.

"Erin, you are not going to like this, but we need to get to the bottom of this and get you admitted to the hospital immediately," he explained.

"Where do I go when I get there?" I asked.

"No, I do not want you driving," he said.

He called our longtime family friend Nancy to see if she would pick me up. Nancy worked with Dr. Rossi and had known me since I was six months old.

Ironically, I had just gotten off the phone with Nancy. I thought she was calling me that morning because she heard I had had a seizure, but she had no idea and was actually calling to see if I could be a speaker at an event in May. When I answered, she thought she had called the wrong number because I didn't sound like my usual, enthusiastic self.

This was not what I wanted, but, if it would bring the happy, passionate person I loved to be back, I would do anything. I got out of my pajamas, packed a few things for the hospital, and called my younger sister to let her know what was going on. I asked her to call our parents, who were both at work.

As we drove to the hospital in Chicago, I described to Nancy that I knew my seizure medication was behind my mood change. She explained that, because I was suicidal, they would have to do an assessment on me when I got to the ER to approve me to go to the neurological floor instead of the psychiatric unit. Nancy had her own experiences in the ER with her daughter and said that we would probably be in there for hours.

She was such a wonderful family friend to be there for me during that difficult time, willing to spend several hours in the ER with me. There were moms with crying babies, senior citizens, and even a man that walked into the ER with a knife attached to his belt who sat down just two feet from us. Nancy and I both saw it and she immediately got on her phone and texted me, "Knife!" For the first time in nearly two weeks, I smiled and could not look at Nancy as I felt I was going to laugh.

It seemed to take forever, and, just when I sensed they were about to call me, I heard my name being called over the intercom to come to the nurses' station in the ER. When I walked up, they said I had a phone call. I thought that was very strange and had no idea who it would be. It ended up being my uncle Bill who had heard through my family that I was rushed to the emergency room. That news certainly traveled fast. He asked how I was doing, and I told him about the seizure and what the drugs did to my thinking. He told me how sorry he was for what I was going through and that he would be praying for me. I thought that was so kind of him to reach out to me so quickly.

Finally, after hours of waiting, I was admitted into a room in the ER. Nancy left when my parents and sister arrived. I ended up spending a total of seven hours in the ER. I underwent a pregnancy test and other random health-screening questions, and eventually a young, good-looking medical student came into the room to inform me that he had to do a psychological evaluation on me. As my parents and sister exited the room, my sister made faces the whole way out behind the medical student's back, quite obviously hinting that she thought the medical student was cute and hoping to make me blush.

I ended up being asked every question you could imagine about my childhood, the abuse I suffered, my vision condition, surgeries I had, teenage years, past depression, my suicide attempt at sixteen, self-injury in high school, the eating disorder that I battled for four years, the epilepsy, and my current suicidal thoughts.

"Some of the same questions you're asking me I was asking teens in my profession as a youth and family therapist when I was on crisis. I did suicidal assessments on youth and never imagined I would ever be asked these questions in my life. This is not who I am. I would never want to take my life. The drugs have clouded my thinking and have caused me to have these dark, suicidal thoughts. Read the warning signs for the drug Keppra. It says it all over how it can cause someone to become suicidal. If you knew me outside my current state of mind, I am a super passionate, determined woman ready to change the world who was on *Oprah* last month, and I am getting my own law passed in Illinois," I said to him. Looking back, he probably thought I was nuts saying I was on *Oprah* and getting my own law passed.

"I need to get back to my happy, determined self as soon as possible. I have to testify this month on Erin's Law. I can't miss it, and I can't do it without my passionate drive, which is currently on empty. That passionate voice is what convinces lawmakers," I told him.

"For all you have endured, you sure have conquered and accomplished a lot in your life. You are certainly resilient," he said.

"Thank you, but I have a whole lot more to accomplish, and this seizure drug is really slowing me down."

"How did you recover from anorexia after four years of it?" he asked.

"I recovered on my own. After getting down to ninety-two pounds, everyone was getting on my case. I just stopped restricting food and excessively working out," I said.

"You were never hospitalized for it? Never in any eating disorder support groups?"

"No, never."

I could tell he wasn't convinced I did not still battle anorexia.

"I fell into the eating disorder because I had never had control in my childhood, and it gave me control. After having my first seizure, it scared me so much, and I thought anorexia had something to do with it. When I had the seizure, I lost all control of my life and realized I needed to give up wanting control and give it to God. He is in control of our lives; we are not. So I began eating more regularly. I want ten kids and you can't have children if you have an eating disorder."

"Ten kids! Wow!" A look of shock came across his face.

Once again, I was probably making myself sound crazy.

"Well, I know I won't get ten kids, but I love children and want to have a big family," I said.

After we finished the psychological evaluation, more lab work was done, and then they brought me dinner.

A certified psychiatrist eventually came in and my family stepped out to go get dinner themselves. She asked me a bunch more questions with the medical student standing behind her. I eventually told them that I didn't plan to act on my suicidal thoughts and had to promise that anytime I was feeling suicidal, I would tell somebody immediately on my hospital floor since they were going to allow me to be on the neurological floor instead of the psych unit. However, I was told because I was suicidal, I would have a psychiatrist checking on me daily while I was in the hospital.

"I can't even believe I am having this conversation with both of you. I wish you both knew the real me who is full of so much energy and life. I promise, if these empty, sad, dark, depressing feelings make me start having more suicidal thoughts, I will tell someone the same way

I told my mother. I know once they get me off this drug that is making me go out of my mind, I will be back to my cheerful, energetic self."

They did require that a family member stay with me at all times, sleep at the hospital with me, and that I couldn't be alone at any time for my own safety.

Finally, after seven hours in the ER, I was brought up to the neurological floor of the hospital, where I eventually said good-bye to my parents. My sister would be staying the night with me. My dad came over to my bed before leaving and hugged me.

"Erin, the world needs you. Don't forget that," he said.

I hugged him back. "Dad, this isn't me. It is the drugs doing it to me. I want the light switch to go back on and go back to saving children instead of saving myself. Don't worry about me."

My mother kissed me and told me how much she loved me.

"I love you both," I said. "Don't worry about me. We will get this all straightened out. My passion will come back on and you will have your determined, outspoken daughter back again in no time."

I hated it when my parents worried about me, and I knew how worried they were. I also knew I had to focus on getting myself back on my feet and to try not to take care of their anxiety and worries. I had done that too much in my life, protecting my parents from being in pain from what I endured. I knew now I had to take care of myself.

I spent the next hour hooked up to yet another EEG to record my brain activity and to monitor any spiking or firing in my brain. This was nothing new since I had done it twice before. Then the next step for the doctors was to start lowering my dosage of Keppra very slowly. The first night I didn't end up going to bed until 1:00 AM and I woke up at 4:00 AM. I got little sleep because I was so uncomfortable with all the wires attached to my head and the IV needle coming out of my arm, which was hurting. I also have issues with sleeping in hospitals.

It reminds me of when I was forced to stay at the hospital when I was seven years old after putting my hand through the window.

I was trying to fall back asleep, but, at 6:00 AM, a man entered my room and said he was a psychiatrist.

"Do you mind if I ask you a few questions?

I was thinking to myself, *Why are you in here so early? I just want to sleep, since I tossed and turned all night.*

He started asking me about depression, my past, suicidal thoughts, and then asked, "Who is our current president? What day is it? Repeat the three words I am giving you. Do you hear voices? What were the three words I told you to repeat?" I was on a roll, answering all his questions correctly, and then he asked me what one hundred minus seven was. I said ninety-two. My sister woke up to him asking me all the questions. After he left, my sister looked at me.

"Erin, one hundred minus seven isn't ninety-two, it's ninety-three." We both burst out laughing.

"I didn't even catch it. I wonder if he did? Well, one thing hasn't changed; I still can't do math. Then again, he *is* asking me at six in the morning and math is the furthest thing from my mind," I told her.

As I sat in my hospital bed watching television approximately an hour after the psychiatrist came into the room, a nurse appeared at my door and came in to take my vital signs. *Good Morning America* was playing on the television, and suddenly a story came on saying, "Reality TV stars who have committed suicide."

The nurse looked at my sister and me. "I just don't get people that would want to kill themselves. Like, seriously, how can life be that bad and who would have the balls to actually kill themselves? I sure couldn't even think of doing something crazy like that to myself," she said.

I couldn't believe what I was hearing, nor could I even look at my sister, because I knew that the same thing was going through her mind that was going through mine. All I was thinking was *Lady, you have no idea who you are talking to.* The other nurses I dealt with all knew the side effects I was having from my seizure medication. I was very offended and tried to hide it from the nurse. I so badly wanted to say, "You might want to be careful what you say." Instead, I responded with, "Well, sometimes people don't have control, like when a side effect to a drug starts making them have suicidal thoughts." I hoped this would clue her in without my needing to be direct.

When she walked out, my sister just looked at me. "I can't believe she just said that," she said.

"Watch her go read my chart now and see the reasons why I was admitted."

This was just another example of why people need to think before they speak. You just never know who you are talking to and what they have been through. She was definitely unprofessional.

I always thought I had to find happiness through someone other than myself. It was like that person was holding on to it and I couldn't be happy until I discovered just who that person was. I searched for it in my family, friends, therapists, and teachers. I thought that maybe it would come from the man I would end up marrying. I would come to discover, however, that I was looking in all the wrong places. I needed to look inside myself. It was in there all along. I just had to discover how to keep it.

Happiness is a personal choice. If you want happiness in life and don't have it, find out what or who is holding you back. I learned not to look to others for happiness. With a little soul searching, I discovered that I had allowed the people who hurt me in my life to continue to steal another day of my happiness. I looked in the mirror and said to myself, *I cannot give them another day of my happiness.*

They have already taken far too many days, weeks, months, and years.
The answers lie within.

So you might be wondering how to transition from depression
to happiness. Well, if you are clinically depressed, it may be best to
be treated with medication. However, most people find themselves
depressed at some point in their lives due to a specific incident or a
number of incidents. The change doesn't happen overnight, but there
is a little step you must address to get to there. Okay, it isn't a little
step. It is actually a rather large step. It is the process of forgiving those
who have hurt you, even if they have not admitted any wrongdoing
or offered an apology.

To make the process even easier for you, you can just forgive them
in your heart and not even make contact with them. By continuing
to harbor hatred, anger, and bitterness toward your enemies, you are
giving them another day of your happiness and joy. You realize in the
process of forgiveness that it is the greatest gift you can give yourself.
You discover freedom in forgiving. As I've stated before, through
forgiveness, you end up releasing a prisoner, and that prisoner isn't
the person who hurt you; that prisoner is you. You just need to turn
that key and let yourself out.

I have forgiven both the man that raped me and the one that
abused me. I cannot carry hatred in my heart for them. It is toxic
and unhealthy for me. I will not allow room for that in my heart and
soul, nor give them another day of my happiness.

Without forgiving those who had hurt me, I realized that I stayed
stuck in that hauntingly dark and depressing place. I was trapped.
Forgiveness led me to peace and a path of moving forward to discovering my potential and achieving all that I believe in. I suddenly found
myself waking up every morning thanking God for the little things
in life that we often take for granted. I found myself in my car often

saying out loud to God, "Thank you for giving me the sun and blue skies today." At night, I often look out the window and thank God for the stars and the moon as well. The moon has a special meaning to me with God. Throughout my childhood when I carried dark secrets that often happened at night, I looked to the moon to talk to God. It was a source of light and comfort for me in such a dark world.

I remember standing by a window once when I was locked in an upstairs bedroom on Christmas Eve with my cousin. He was coming toward me to do what he had done so many times before. I focused on the moon and was praying my heart out to God, praying to Him to rescue me in this moment. Just as my cousin was walking toward me, there was a knock at the door. I wanted to shout out in that moment, "Thank you, God!"

Seconds earlier, fear had consumed me. Now, a sense of relief washed over me. It was as if God had sent someone to my rescue, an uncle who made his way upstairs and knocked on the door just as my cousin was about to make his move. God was letting me know He heard me and that He was there. During a time of extreme fear, I felt God's amazing grace.

"What are you doing up here?" my uncle asked.

"Just chasing each other around," my cousin said.

Sure, you were about to assault me, I thought to myself.

Unfortunately, my cousin would go on to molest me two more times that Christmas Eve. Once, in a dark room with several other cousins and my sisters, he was able to get his hands down my pants. The second time occurred after my parents left early to put the presents out. As his parents drove my sisters and me back home, he molested me the whole car ride home.

As I laid in a hospital bed hooked up to a bunch of wires that were recording brain activity while I was on suicide watch, I found myself praying all these dark, negative thoughts would go away and the happy, joyful, determined, energetic, and passionate person I knew would return to me. I wanted to feel the energy that I normally felt to go out and conquer a silent epidemic.

This was just another obstacle I was faced with, but, deep down, my faith was so strong that I knew the darkness that consumed me would lift and the joy and happiness I had come to know so well would return to me. I just needed to remain patient and faithful. I didn't fear I was going to stay suicidal. I knew I would be back on my feet in no time to testify on Erin's Law once again at the capitol in Illinois.

I slept most of the day on Wednesday until midafternoon when my doctor came in with another doctor to describe the side effects of the new drug he was putting me on called Lyrica. The first words out of his mouth about side effects were weight gain. That is difficult news to hear for someone who once battled anorexia.

"No, I won't be put on a drug that ends up making me gain a bunch of weight," I said.

"I tell all my patients I put on Lyrica to diet and work out," he said.

"You don't understand. I can't put myself on diets. You know I suffered for four years with anorexia, and, if you get me dieting, it will turn into obsessing over what I am eating, restricted eating, weighing myself every day, and I will eventually have a problem that I never want to battle in my life again, because it was so hard to stop obsessing over every calorie."

"Erin, you are in control here. We work as a team," he said.

I sure wasn't feeling in control. I felt like everything was in the hands of the doctors. There was so much fear in me with everything that was going on that I didn't even want to allow myself to think about it. Thoughts of having more seizures, side effects, wondering whether this new drug would work or not, how my body would respond, and wondering if the light switch would turn back on to my joyful self all ran through my mind. Reflecting back on this moment, I was still not in the right frame of mind and needed to remind myself to give this to God. I knew he was in control, and he had a hand in all of this.

I was still feeling very tired, unmotivated, and depressed throughout the course of the day. With my nurse looking on, my doctor began to talk to me about my mood.

"Erin, you are not the outgoing, energetic, bright-eyed woman I have seen in my office." His nurse agreed. "Have you been having any suicidal thoughts today?"

"No," I told him.

"Would you be honest and tell someone if you were feeling that way?" he asked.

"I promise I will."

Before leaving, he told me they were going to continue to monitor my mood and brain for seizure activity.

Later in the day, another doctor came in to speak with me because I was about to get my first dose of Lyrica.

"Have you been informed of the side effects Lyrica can cause?" he asked.

"A few; can you go over all of them with me?" I asked.

The first words out of his mouth were weight gain as well. For somebody like me, this was especially difficult to hear for the second time. Because of my loss of control early in life, I went down a very destructive path, searching for control through self-injury and anorexia. I had no idea what was coming or if it would be a seizure that would take my control from me again. I had to learn to adjust and adapt to this brain injury, give up control, and give it to God.

When I had seizures, I had no control over the situation. However, I came to realize that if these drugs were going to keep me from having

them, which I could not stop on my own, then I knew how important it was to learn to accept my condition and take the medication.
Unfortunately, now that I had experienced more than one seizure, I
was officially given the diagnosis of epilepsy.

I was hooked up to twenty-five wires for three days, and I had to
stay in bed at all times unless I had to use the bathroom. Then I had
to bring with me several cords and a black case that carried them all.
I was also unable to shower this entire time. I certainly couldn't offend
myself, since I couldn't smell. After three days of recording brain
waves, my doctors did see epileptic activity, which is often referred to
as spiking and firing in the brain, but they recorded no actual seizures.

I was informed that I could have a seizure without even knowing
it. There are different kinds of seizures, and the two I have had in my
life have been full tonic-clonic seizures, which left me in pain for days.

My doctor lowered the Keppra I was taking, the drug that had made
me suicidal, to 1,500 mgs a day, dropping it 1,000 mgs. The 2,500 mg
dose was too powerful for my small body. My doctor had continued
to increase it every time I had an aura over the course of six months.
The goal now was to get me off the drug completely.

Doctors tried telling me in the hospital that it might not be the drug
Keppra that was doing this to me. There was a chance that when I had
the last seizure, the shaking in my head could have caused a shift in
my mood, leaving me very depressed and suicidal. While they may
be doctors and have gone to school for a very long time, nobody, and
I mean nobody, knows their body better than the person living in it. I
knew this had nothing to do with the seizure and had everything to do
with the drug Keppra. I am a very observant person, especially when
it comes to my body and how I am feeling physically and mentally. I
noticed my mood change immediately after the drug increase.

"How is your mood? How do you feel? What are your interests?"

I was woken out of a deep sleep on Thursday morning by the same psychiatrist who visited me the previous morning.

"I am tired. I am interested in going back to sleep; my mood is starting to feel a lot better," I told him.

My mother had spent the night with me and got to witness the psychiatrist questioning this time around.

"You really need to follow up with psychiatric care and therapy when you get discharged. Would you like to see someone from Rush or someone back home?" he asked.

I told him what he wanted to hear. "Sure, okay, I will follow up with someone when I get home," I looked at my mom when he walked out.

"I am not following up with anyone. I will be myself in a matter of days."

"Erin, maybe he is right. Maybe it would be good for you to talk to someone about having epilepsy and what it does to you. You are dealing with a lot," she stated.

"Mom, all I need to do is get off this drug that is making me go out of my mind, return to my happy, energetic self, and get back to passing Erin's Law. I don't need therapy. I have had enough of that in my life."

Within days of the hospital lowering the Keppra, I started to feel like myself again, which I knew I would. The darkness soon turned to a foggy state of mind, and the fog soon turned to light. Unfortunately, once my mental state of mind started to feel good again, I began having physical pains in the center of my chest. It got so bad that I could no longer eat or drink—not even water. I didn't have a sore throat or shooting pain. It was just a terrible, awful stabbing pain in the center of my chest when food went down. When doctors heard I couldn't even eat or drink, they began treating me for acid reflux, which I have never had in my life. I have never had any type of chest pain.

I had three friends come and visit me in the hospital that Thursday night. One of those friends, Becky, brought coloring books, gossip magazines, and a goofy reindeer that you are supposed to put in water to watch it grow. While my mom and sister went and grabbed dinner in Chicago to get out of the hospital, my friend Becky and I talked. Becky filled a container with water and dropped the reindeer in. When my mom and sister came back, they were laughing, and, of course, my sister loved it. She starts celebrating Christmas two months before the actual day. I said, "Great, the psychiatrist is really going to think I am out of my mind now, and I will never get out of here."

Every night in the hospital, I woke up when a nurse came in to take my vital signs. This night was no different, as I awoke to my arm being lifted. I opened my eyes, and standing over me, putting a blood-pressure cuff on my arm, was a bald African=American male nurse. Panic and fear swept over me. I quickly shut my eyes as terrible images began to play out in my mind. Flashbacks of the bald African-American man who raped me as a child haunted me. Confined to a hospital bed with more than two dozen wires attached to my head, these images made me want to start pulling out the wires and take off running. The nurse had been gone more than ten minutes, yet I was still trapped in this flashback. I kept blinking my eyes, trying to make it stop. The grounding techniques I learned through years of therapy that had helped me escape flashbacks in the past were of no use to me stuck in this hospital room. Finally, I heard over the hospital floor intercom "EEG 316" repeated several times. This code is what sends the nurses running to a room because someone pushed their emergency seizure button. Hearing the commotion brought me out of a terrible memory and back to the third floor of a hospital in Chicago. I am positive my blood pressure that night was recorded as being the highest it had been during my entire stay at the hospital.

For the past two days, the psychiatrist had been saying I needed psychiatric follow-up care. But Friday morning, after seeing my drastic mood change compared to when I first came in on Tuesday, he said, "I don't think you need psychiatric follow-up care."

"Well, she is growing a reindeer in water behind you," my sister blurted out.

He turned around and looked in the container and then looked at me.

"On that note, I think it is time to take you to the fourth floor," which was the psych unit. All three of us were laughing. We had him laughing all the way out the door as he said good-bye.

I was so ready to go home and grateful that the rooms were private. That was the one nice thing. No stranger was sleeping next to me with only a curtain dividing us. By Sunday, they cleared me to go home after six days in the hospital. It was nice to come home and sleep in my own bed. The feelings of happiness, drive, passion, determination, and motivation inside me were all back, which I knew they would be.

I can honestly say those first two weeks in November 2010 were two of the darkest weeks I have ever had in my life. You just never know what life will throw at you. I now had to learn to accept that I did have epilepsy. As with the shame and stigma I had overcome from being sexually abused and having a learning disability, I had to overcome the stigma associated with epilepsy. Fifty million people worldwide understand what living with epilepsy is like. That is how many deal with it day in and day out. Epilepsy affects more Americans than Parkinson's disease, Lou Gehrig's disease, and multiple sclerosis combined.

The difference between my epilepsy and the sexual abuse I suffered was that I had to come to terms with the fact that I was a survivor of sexual abuse and was never going to be abused again, but epilepsy would be a part of my life forever, unless, by the grace of God, he healed me. With faith, anything is possible.

I won't let epilepsy control my life. I often get asked, "Are you afraid you are going to have a seizure onstage while speaking?" "Doesn't it worry you to travel alone?" "What if you have a seizure?" So many questions are aimed at how epilepsy affects my life. Guess what? I am not afraid at all. I won't give epilepsy that kind of control over my life and let it stop me from all that I plan to achieve. I never once had any fear about having a seizure while onstage speaking. Yes, it is possible that it could happen. But guess what? It wouldn't be the end of the world. I cannot spend my life worrying about the "what ifs." I choose to be optimistic. I know that I will win any battle I might face against epilepsy. I will always have people in my life there to support me and get me through it, picking me right back up again, ready to conquer what I set out to do next.

I hold out hope that researchers will find a cure not only for me but for all who suffer from epilepsy. According to the Epilepsy Foundation, epilepsy affects 3 million Americans. Approximately 200,000 new cases occur each year. Ten percent of the American population will experience a seizure in their lifetime, and it is the fourth most common neurologic condition.

Some days are easier than others. I still get auras. Some are stronger than others. I am now at a place where I have gotten the panic attacks under control. I take one day at a time, and I know whatever happens in my life, God will be there walking right alongside me, helping me with my struggles, decisions, mission, and purpose he has for me.

I won't let anything stop me. I didn't allow my abusers to keep me silent. I didn't allow a learning disability to stop me from going to college and getting my master's degree. I certainly will not allow epilepsy to stop me from getting in front of lawmakers and testifying state by state to protect children from sexual abuse.

I believe we are all born with a purpose—a purpose some of us discover early on in life while others discover it later. We are all on this earth for some reason or another. If you haven't found your purpose, I highly suggest you sit down and do some soul searching. The way I found happiness inside is the same way I found my purpose. The answers lie within. I can promise you that. Don't let anyone or anything stop you from anything you want to achieve. If you have faith in yourself, anything is possible.

"You don't have enough faith," Jesus told them.
"I tell you the truth, if you had faith even as small
as a mustard seed, you could say to this mountain,
'Move from here to there,' and it would move.
Nothing would be impossible."

—Matthew 17:20 (New Living Translation)

Chapter 18

Back on Course

I BELIEVE THAT IF YOU
SHOW PEOPLE THE PROBLEMS
AND YOU SHOW THEM THE
SOLUTIONS THEY WILL
BE MOVED TO ACT.

—*Bill Gates*

A week after being admitted to the hospital, I suddenly felt all the passion, determination, happiness, and joy back in my life again. My sister drove me down to the capital of Illinois, Springfield, where I met with both the Senate and House of Representative sponsors of Erin's Law. We entered a room at the Illinois State Capitol where Erin's Law would be heard. The room was filled with people and representatives.

As we took our seats, waiting for the representatives to come in and take theirs, Representative Mitchell turned to me. He said, "See the representative, second row, three seats in on the left? She is Suzi Bassi and she will be completely against this bill. She will speak that loud and clear to the legislators when we open it up for discussion. She has said no to school mandates for years and she knows this will eventually become a mandated bill. So don't worry about her since we already know she will oppose this bill. Focus on convincing the rest of the representatives."

I sat there thinking, *No I am not just going to give up on Representative Suzi Bassi. I am going to make it a point to use my testimony to convince her and make eye contact with her several times as I testify.* Representative Mitchell's advice to ignore her only made me want to focus on her.

Unfortunately I had concerns more pressing than Representative Bassi. A woman from another bill spent an entire hour testifying, taking up all the allowed time for bills to be heard that day. They would hear the rest tomorrow. Since my doctor ordered that I not drive, my sister took the day off to drive me there. We had driven three and a half hours and now I was being told I couldn't testify on the law I had dedicated my life to. Representative Jerry Mitchell ran up to the microphone and asked me to follow him.

"I wouldn't ask this, but I have Erin Merryn here who cannot come back tomorrow and who was just released from the hospital to be here to testify on a bill near and dear to her heart. If we can just give her a couple minutes to testify. . . . We can run the bill tomorrow for the vote, if you can just let her testify."

The Speaker of the House, Michael Madigan, happened to walk into the room as people were exiting. He gave them the go-ahead to allow me to testify. I knew to keep it short and to the point.

I grew up in an Illinois public school. I learned tornado drills, bus drills, fire drills, not to talk to strangers, and not to go looking for that little lost puppy. I went through the DARE program and was taught the eight ways to say no to drugs. I am sure many of you have children that have gone through this program and were warned not to say yes to drugs when approached and told not to go looking for that lost puppy. The one question that didn't come in my childhood was on safe touch, unsafe touch, safe secrets, unsafe secrets, and the eight ways on how to get away and how to tell today, and because that message never came to me, from the ages of six to eight, I was sexually abused and raped by my best friend's uncle. From the ages of eleven to thirteen, I was molested at the hands of a family member. Because nobody was giving me the message on how to speak up about sexual abuse, on what safe touch is, on how to put a face and voice on this, I stayed silent and listened to my perpetrators. And I am urging you to listen to Senate Bill 2843 and pass it, because what it will do is educate children in the schools on what failed me in my education in Illinois. By educating children on sexual abuse in schools at the elementary level, you are giving them the tools and knowledge to speak up and reach out and tell somebody if they are being abused, unlike my childhood, where I couldn't put a face and voice on it because nobody was giving me that message. My perpetrators were telling me that "this is our little secret." Please, I urge you to pass Senate Bill 2843, because as I say, we cannot stop these sexual predators. They will always exist! So why not put an extra layer of protection around children to protect them? Thank you. I won't take any more of your time.

Two days later the front-page headline of the story covered from the *Daily Herald* newspaper reporter Kim Pohl read: Erin's Law Moving Closer to Reality. This is an excerpt from the article:

She spoke for just three minutes, but Erin Merryn's powerful testimony Tuesday to the Illinois House Education Committee about the sexual abuse she suffered at the hands of two entrusted caretakers quieted chatter and induced tears.

So moved by her chilling words and charge to teach children "how to get away and how to tell today," 30 legislators requested they be added as co-sponsors to Erin's Law, which passed 110–0 the following day.

"It's like Erin said: Kids had tornado training and fire drills but they never learned about safe touch and unsafe touch," said state Rep. Suzie Bassi, a Palatine Republican.

Also a victim of sexual abuse, Bassi became emotional hearing Merryn speak. "This gives little ones tools to be able to protect themselves or tell another adult," she said.

Her testimony before the state panel almost didn't happen. Discussion on another bill took up the session's allotted hour and the committee recessed. It took state Rep. Jerry Mitchell, a bill sponsor and Rock Falls Republican, to run up to the microphone and implore members to listen to Merryn, who couldn't return the next day.

"I threw a temper tantrum, which I don't often do," said Mitchell, who can recall the entire committee requesting to be added as sponsors only two times in the 16 years he's been in office. "It's a topic that we've shied away from for too long."

Then the most amazing thing happened. Representative Suzie Bassi, who Representative Mitchell had warned me about as opposing this bill, did the complete opposite as he had predicted. Fighting through tears as the vote was being taken, she publicly disclosed to everyone in the room that she, herself, was a survivor of childhood sexual abuse and that she completely supported the law. It touched her personally, allowing her to see the importance of what Erin's Law would do for children: give them a voice to speak up and not give sex offenders the ability to silence our children.

Remember how I had a state senator tell me I would never get this law passed? I made the choice to move forward and find someone who would support it because I believed in what I was going after. I didn't want to see another generation of children go uneducated. Now we had both the Senate and House in Illinois all voting yes in support of educating our children on sexual abuse prevention in schools. Erin's Law never received a single vote against the law in the state of Illinois. It was all left up to Illinois governor Pat Quinn to sign.

Finally, the day I had worked so hard for had arrived. On February 14, 2011, Governor Quinn signed Erin's Law. It was such a feeling of accomplishment. All my hard work and determination had paid off. I ignored the doubters and got the job done. However, the work wasn't over. This was just the beginning. This part of the law didn't yet mandate sexual abuse prevention in the schools. It urged schools to adopt a policy to teach it but didn't yet hold them responsible to teach it. The focus was to build the task force that the law mandated to do research and report back to the governor with recommendations on the issues. It was a start.

I was appointed to be on the task force along with eighteen others who were highly qualified to work on making the recommendations. The group included law enforcement, state board of education members, principals, superintendents, college professors, child abuse prevention specialists, social workers, and researchers, to name a few.

Members of the task force needed to be individuals who were actively involved in the fields of the prevention of child abuse, neglect, and child welfare. The appointed members also needed to reflect the geographic diversity of the state. The task force would have a presiding officer elected by a majority of the task force members. The group would meet at the request of the presiding officer, and they would make recommendations for reducing child sexual abuse in Illinois. In making those recommendations, the task force was required to:

- Gather information concerning child sexual abuse throughout the state.

- Receive reports and testimony from individuals, state and local agencies, community-based organizations, and other public and private organizations.

- Create goals for state policy that would prevent child sexual abuse.

- Submit a final report with its recommendations to the Office of the Governor and the General Assembly by January 1, 2012.

The recommendations could include proposals for specific statutory changes and methods to foster cooperation among state agencies and between the state and local government. The task force was to consult with employees of the Department of Children and Family Services, the Criminal Justice Information Agency, the Department of State Police, the Illinois State Board of Education, and any other state agency or department as necessary to accomplish its responsibilities under this section. The members of the task force would serve without compensation and were not to be reimbursed for their expenses. Upon submission of the final report to the Office of the Governor and the General Assembly, the task force would be abolished.

For ten months, the task force met in different locations through-out Illinois. For several hours a day, we would discuss the different aspects of Erin's Law and what our goals were. We created subcommittees: Research, Prevention, Administrator, Teacher, and Parent Committees. My main focus was on the research of the curriculum for schools. Because of the national recognition I received on Erin's Law through my appearance on *Oprah*, I began receiving curriculum, books, and activities from around the country. Research backing up the curriculum was crucial for recommendations.

It is not only important that we educate students. Administrators and teachers also need to be educated and trained on how to identify signs of a child who is being abused and how to properly handle a situation if a child comes forward. I have heard horror stories of educators handling an abused child coming forward the wrong way. They need to be properly educated so these children who disclose being abused in the home don't end back up in the home with the one abusing them.

If schools decide to use teachers, school social workers, or someone else in the school to teach students, they need to have the proper training to teach the material and be comfortable with presenting it. We don't want the wrong people teaching children, which is why educating and training school personnel is so important.

Parents need to be educated as well, and need to be able to follow up with questions at home on the material taught in schools. It is not an easy subject, but it is a subject that has been ignored for far too long in our society, and if it takes someone like me to fight for children to get the education they deserve, I won't allow anything to stop me.

Knowing a child could be empowered with their voice by reporting grooming or a first incident of sexual abuse instead of living in silence for years and enduring years of sexual abuse is worth everything I have put on the line to see this law passed in my home state. When I made the decision to go public, putting a face and voice on sexual abuse by publishing my diary, entitled *Stolen Innocence*, I told myself, *If this book can just help one person find their voice and give them courage, it is worth it.* Since then, I have heard from thousands over the years from people in my own town to the other side of the world. I've heard from people on every continent except Antarctica. Antarctica is probably the only place you could go where you wouldn't find a sex offender on the prowl in search of their next victim to abuse. The letters have poured in with people sharing with me how my books have helped them find their voice, heal, and find hope. Through my own transformation, I showed them that it is possible to rise out of darkness and find the light within.

While writing books and traveling the country for a living, speaking at conferences, schools, and state capitols has been therapeutic; the reason I do it is for those 42 million survivors in America, 3 million of which are children that have been sexually abused. Those 3 million children could fill forty-six national football stadiums. It is a sad reality. They are my driving force.

My mission with Erin's Law did not end with just my home state. I decided to take this law national and see that it passed in all fifty states. I thought to myself, *If I can get this done in my home state of*

Illinois, why not every other state? The children of Illinois are not the only ones who need to be empowered with their voice. So I set the bar really high, with the mission of passing this law in all fifty states, and believe me, I will get it done. I know it sounds like a huge task I am putting on myself, but I am confident it will happen. I won't look the other way and ignore this silent epidemic. Sadly, the world I live in does. I won't continue to allow this message to fall on deaf years. The subject is not widely accepted because we live in a world that looks the other way and acts as if it isn't going on. I am going to continue to wake up society to the reality of the silence thousands of children go to bed with every night, until the only ones who are silenced are the sex offenders themselves.

Chapter 19

Mission Across America

SAFETY AND SECURITY DON'T
JUST HAPPEN; THEY ARE THE RESULT OF
COLLECTIVE CONSENSUS AND PUBLIC
INVESTMENT. WE OWE OUR CHILDREN,
THE MOST VULNERABLE CITIZENS
IN OUR SOCIETY, A LIFE FREE
OF VIOLENCE AND FEAR.

—*Nelson Mandela*

I immediately began reaching out to lawmakers in other states and eventually heard from Senator Ryan McKenna from Missouri, who heard about me from a survivor who wanted Erin's Law to be passed in his state. He was the next senator to introduce my law. I was unable to travel to the capital of Missouri and testify the way I had in Illinois; however, I was asked to send in videotaped testimony. In the video, I reached out to Missouri lawmakers and told them how my innocence was taken and why they should support this law. The video testimony was shown to both the Senate and House.

In April, the Missouri Senate passed it, and, in May 2011, the House passed it. Soon Erin's Law was on the way to the governor's desk in Missouri. Five months after Erin's Law was passed in Illinois, Missouri governor Jay Nixon signed Erin's Law on July 14, 2011. This was just the beginning of my journey. I was making history, and I knew I was one step closer to giving children a voice, something that should have been done long ago.

By 2012, a year after it was signed into law in Illinois, I had made great progress in my mission by reaching out to senators across America in every state. In February, I was asked to testify at the capitol in Indianapolis after Senator Collins sponsored my bill. It was a long day. I was told I would testify at 1:00 PM, but 1:00 PM turned to 3:00 PM, and soon it was 5:30 PM, and I still hadn't testified. After sitting for five hours listening to other bills be voted on, my bill was finally called. The roughly fifty people in the room lost interest in the topics at hand hours earlier. They were chatting, texting on their phones, or playing on their iPads by the time my bill was called.

After Senate sponsor Rogers explained the law, I came to the podium and testified. You could see it in the senators' eyes and body language that they were tired and ready for the day to be over. My sister and her friend were in the room and described how everyone that wasn't paying attention for the past few hours suddenly grew silent. I had their full attention. While my back was to the audience, I could feel all eyes on me as I spoke from the heart. The people in the room were no longer engaged in their online game, reading an e-mail, updating their Facebook status, or sending a tweet on Twitter. I had every senators' attention, too. As I testified, it was so quiet, you could hear a pin drop. After finishing, a senator got on his microphone.

"Ms. Merryn, the Senate sponsor knows I was coming into this vote with plans to vote against this bill, but, after hearing your testimony, you have completely changed my mind, and I see the importance of this bill and what it will do for children. You have my full support, and thank you for sharing your courageous personal testimony. You are a very brave woman."

The Indiana Senate went on to vote 48–0 and the House voted 95–0, all in favor of Erin's Law. Just like Illinois, it never received a single negative vote. In April 2012, Governor Daniels of Indiana signed Erin's Law, making it the third state to pass it. Shortly after Governor Daniels signed it, I heard from Senator Maker in Maine, informing me that Erin's Law passed the Senate and House and was on to the governor's desk. It would later go on to be signed by the governor in Maine in May.

On April 30, 2012, I flew to Albany, New York, the next state to introduce Erin's Law. I went to the capitol to do a press conference on Erin's Law and watch in the chambers as the Senate voted. After an excellent press conference with a lot of media coverage, we walked over to the chambers to watch the voting get under way.

Senator Jeff Klein of Brooklyn, New York, introduced me in the chamber to all the senators: "Today, we have a very special guest in the chamber with us. Someone who has courage and commitment and who has spent the better part of the last year fighting for a very important piece of legislation that she hopes to pass in all fifty states named for her, Erin Merryn's Law. I want to take a couple of moments to share Erin's story. It is certainly a very compelling one. She has gone through great tragedy in her life and has tried to make it into a positive."

Senator Klein went on to describe the story of what I endured as a child and what Erin's Law would do for the children of New York and America. After taking my seat from being recognized in the chambers, Senator Adams stood up to explain his vote:

> I just want to commend young Erin. It is difficult to turn pain into purpose. Often people go internally when they feel a level of pain instead of reaching out and trying to prevent people from experiencing their pain. Stories like this are so profound, and I think it is important that we use our classrooms for more than just teaching one and one equals two and must teach some of the challenges and socialization problems young people will experience. I not only thank you for myself as a senator but as someone who has a son. It is heroes like you that make it possible for legislators not to get so far removed from this comfortable environment we live in. There are real problems out there and real people like you are giving us great solutions. I thank my colleague for this bill and I thank you for doing this. We must make all states in America have this bill in the book.

After Senator Adams spoke, a female senator stood in voting against the bill. Everyone is entitled to their opinion, but this female senator obviously hadn't read the bill correctly, because she went on a rant about sex education. Erin's Law had nothing to do with teaching kids about safe sex. The law has everything to do with teaching kids how to protect their minds, bodies, and innocence from ever being abused. Erin's Law informs kids about the grooming process and to not keep secrets if someone ever does abuse them, a huge difference from what this senator was speaking about, and all of the other senators recognized that it had nothing to do with what she was talking about. After she finished, Senator Savino stood to speak on the bill.

I rise in support of this piece of legislation. I want to say to Erin Merryn, you are a remarkable young woman who has shown tremendous courage where most people would run and hide. As I told you earlier in the press conference, when I was a caseworker in the city's child welfare agency, the most difficult cases were children who were victims of sexual abuse. Their scars were internal, not external. You couldn't look at them and see the bruises and broken bones and evidence of abuse they suffered, but it is a very real suffering millions of children go through, and the really sad reality is these children are victimized by people they love and trust. Family members, people who they look up to, people they would not question.

When we think about the very small children, they have no frame of reference. They don't know what sexual abuse is because they don't know what sex is. They don't know what inappropriate touching is. So we need to educate our children. We need to educate our educators, because as we begin to talk about these things publicly, we will have children who will self-report what is happening in their home, when they are visiting their uncle, or when they see their next-door neighbor. This has to be a collaborative effort about educating children, educating our communities, and trying to cut back on the risk young children face every day at the hands of people they love and know the most. So I want to thank you, Erin, and I want to thank Senator Klein for bringing this legislation forward; hopefully this will be the next state to adopt Erin's Law.

Senator Smith then stood to explain his vote.

To Erin, thank you! That is all I can say to you. Thank you! You are very brave. I don't know how you muster up the strength given what you have been through to do this. But to be so magnanimous in your effort for other people, I know God will continue to bless you and your family. Know that we are going to do the right thing by you. We know how hard this is for you. You probably remember it night after night. I have a daughter myself and I don't know if I could even stand to have her sit here and hear this. This is serious and I hope people understand how serious this is. This is not a matter of you being here other than the fact that you feel this is the right thing to do. I am going to vote yes, and know that I will ask all my colleagues as well as others to do so. God bless you.

Seconds after Senator Smith spoke, they announced the result of the vote: 55 ayes, 1 nay. The bill passed! Applause broke out in the chambers. After the vote was over, I was approached outside the chambers by two male senators who said they were sexually abused as children, too, and that I was right; it is often by someone the child knows. They informed me they both knew their abuser, and it was someone they trusted.

Once again, I was witnessing people of high authority openly sharing that they were survivors. More and more I was witnessing the difference this law could truly bring our nation, and one day the world. We live in a world of people who are hurting and broken. I have turned in my brokenness for change. I can't change the past, but I can change the future, and that is what I focus on. I am living by faith, knowing I have turned my pain into purpose for the protection of children from the suffering I endured as a child.

By May 2012, Illinois, Missouri, Indiana, and Maine had all signed Erin's Law. Unfortunately, trying to convince lawmakers in every state to pass this law was not going to always go as planned. I knew just

trying to get Erin's Law passed in my home state would bring challenges. So moving forward on a national level, I knew the road ahead
would not be a simple one, and there would be lawmakers who would
not support my vision of this law. As you have learned by now, I don't
give up that easy. I accomplish what I go after. If that means a state
votes down Erin's Law one year, that doesn't mean I am not coming
back the next year with a push to get it passed. And I will be back year
after year if I have to, until it gets passed. I never gave up on passing
algebra; I won't give up on passing Erin's Law nationally.

After a successful outcome on April 30, 2012, with the New York
Senate passing Erin's Law in June, the New York House Education
Committee failed to vote on the bill because there was debate about
the law being an unfunded mandate to schools. We had already proved
and stated in a press conference in New York that there are already
nonprofit programs that go into schools at no charge and teach this
material in New York schools, but, because it is not mandated, it
doesn't get into all schools.

In our final task force report in Illinois, we discovered through our
research that there are several ways for schools that do not have funding to get this material taught to students. There are many prevention
educators in nonprofit programs who are willing to go into the schools
to teach children, but schools are just not willing to bring them in.
Funding is an unexceptional excuse and makes me sick every time I
hear it brought up. Don't put a price tag on a child's innocence. It is
worth every penny to preserve and protect it.

If America can spend trillions of dollars on a war in Iraq, why
would we not spend money to educate and protect our children from
the war going on against them in our own backyards? That is why
we call this a silent epidemic, because that is exactly what it is, and,
until something like Erin's Law wakes up society, it is only going to

get worse from this generation to the next. We protect our country when we are under attack, so why are we not protecting our children from being attacked? Money is an excuse for those opposed to this legislation. This is much deeper than money; this has to do with a society we live in that doesn't want to accept that this evil is really happening and is spreading like wildfire across this world, waiting to steal the innocence of yet another child.

These are the children that end up spending years in therapy trying to regain the ability to trust again, trying to find the confidence to talk through what happened. There are those who've turned to alcohol and drugs to cope with their abuse who are now finding themselves in rehab. There are children, teens, and adults who have fallen into eating disorders and are currently in inpatient treatment centers due to the sexual abuse they suffered. There are sexual abuse survivors working the streets as prostitutes who have lost all respect for themselves, allowing men to use them for sex. Putting an end to sexual abuse early through education can be lifesaving and prevent many from falling down an extremely dangerous path.

Research shows it is better to have staff inside the school like the teacher, school social worker, or school psychologist teaching the curriculum to children. That way, if a child is taught at the start of the school year and halfway through the year someone touches them inappropriately, they know where to locate that teacher or other school personnel and are able to report it immediately. Every school is different, and many would feel more comfortable having it be a prevention educator that has been going into schools for years teaching children.

Hearing the news that New York members of the House Education Committee failed to vote on Erin's Law was disappointing. I wish I was there when they decided not to vote on it. I would say to all who were in disagreement with the law, "Shame on you for putting a price tag on children's innocence, minds, and bodies."

In May and June 2013, we were back at it again in New York. Once again it passed in the Senate with full support but for one. The House Education Committee chair was refusing to have the bill heard for a second year in a row. She would not bring it up for vote nor return my phone calls or others. She had always voted down school mandates and that wasn't about to change. I don't know how someone could be against giving a child a voice from a life of abuse. I am asking for an hour out of a school year. Is that really that difficult? I think students can miss a recess or art class once a year to protect them. When the chairwoman refused to return my calls, I began rallying many people to take action and had an excellent lobbyist, BJ, putting forth a great deal of effort. I also reached out to actress Julianna Margulies, whom I had met in late 2012. She fully supported my mission with Erin's Law. When Julianna heard her state of New York was refusing to vote, she was furious and asked, "Who the heck would be against this?"

In a press release, Julianna stated, "Erin's Law will give children a fighting chance, a voice, and the tools to help protect themselves. It should be passed in all fifty states. Common sense—it's as simple as that."

Assembly sponsor Jeff Dinowitz said, "This is a very simple, commonsense piece of legislation that could have a positive impact on many young New Yorkers. A little education can go a long way. I applaud Erin Merryn for having the courage to speak out and be a leader on this important issue. I will continue to work to help make this bill a law."

Julianna Margulies reached out to Mayor Bloomberg to get him to support it and asked how we could move forward in getting it passed. Mayor Bloomberg was in full support after speaking with Julianna, but, with just two weeks left before the bill would die, he felt they needed more time and felt we would have a greater chance in 2014. Julianna was fired up over the assembly refusing to hear the bill. Over the phone she said, "Erin, while it might not get passed this year, it sure as hell will get passed next year. I will make sure of it."

On June 24, 2013, the Erin's Law bill died for the second year in New York. We have a great game plan going for 2014 to get Erin's Law passed in New York. With Julianna Margulies, Mayor Bloomberg, Katie Couric, and many legislators supporting the bill, it will get done. I was also informed that Governor Cuomo supports this law. The assembly of New York can't get rid of me. They haven't yet realized who they are dealing with. I am a woman who accomplishes what she goes after, no matter how many tries it takes. Don't worry, New Yorkers, I promise we will get it done.

I have discovered that it helps when legislators hear me speak directly with them on the importance of this law. It makes it more personal coming from a survivor. Usually, when I testify, I have great success in opening up lawmakers' minds as to why this law is so important. There will come a day when I will be saying that New York is the next state to pass Erin's Law.

I know New York will not be the last state either. I will have to fight harder to pass Erin's Law. There will be more to come and we will deal with that as the time comes. I knew all along that in attempting to pass Erin's Law in every state, there would be hurdles to face.

On July 17, 2012, I embarked on the next state to tackle Erin's Law, the state of Michigan. There was a hearing for me to testify at in the capitol on July 18. It was interesting how I got connected with Michigan. It wasn't one of those states where I blasted a letter to legislators and was getting a response from one who wanted to introduce the law. In 2007, I stood up in my cousin's wedding. My cousin had a friend standing up in her wedding who had a sister that worked for Michigan Senator Proos. The rest is history.

I spent the day before testifying meeting with reporters for a press conference on the law. With me at the press conference was Senator Proos, the one introducing the law, and executive director of the Berrien County Children's Advocacy Center, Jamie Rossow. Together, we discussed the importance of this issue and answered questions from reporters. There was great media coverage of Erin's Law for Michigan, and it was being heard in homes across the state.

The morning of July 18 began very early. Senator Proos picked me up from my hotel at 5:20 AM, and we drove an hour to Kalamazoo for a live news interview. I sat at the news desk and discussed the importance of Erin's Law. Afterward, we had another hour of driving before we arrived at the capitol in Lansing, Michigan.

Once at the capitol, I met with the other Senate sponsors of Erin's Law. We discussed the plans of the day and the hope that I would get a few minutes with the governor to discuss the law. I then sat on the Senate floor and did several radio interviews with Michigan stations about the purpose of Erin's Law. At eleven that morning, I entered a room to testify to the Senate Health Policy Committee. As I go state to state testifying, it is a scene that I am becoming all too familiar with. There is a table facing a bunch of legislators and a room of people behind me. I speak from the heart and have been doing this long enough to know just what to say. I've never used notes or have written testimony.

Senator Proos and I were called up by the chairman of the committee. He said, "I appreciate very much my colleagues taking up these bills, Mr. Chairman. I know time is short, and I think that the testimony that Erin will provide today will give great context for the bills that my colleagues on the committee and myself have sponsored.

So with that, I'd like to introduce Erin Merryn, who will give a little bit of background on the purposes for us discussing Erin's Law today."

As I had shared my story with so many others, I testified to the committee that day:

> Thanks, Senator Proos. I appreciate your time today. I am here to talk to you about a very delicate issue that society often sweeps under the rug and we pretend it doesn't exist, but I guarantee you that every single one of you in this room knows somebody that has been affected by this; even if you don't know who, someone in your life has been affected by sexual abuse the way I was in my childhood.
>
> If you were to look at these pictures of me, happy, smiling as a young, little girl at the age of six, seven, eight, eleven, twelve, and thirteen, you would never know the horror I was enduring during my childhood. From six, seven, and eight, I was sexually abused and raped at the hands of my best friend's uncle, who lived in my best friend's home up the street from me. Did I go home and tell? No, I didn't. I kept it a secret, because he threatened that he would come get me. He knew where I lived.
>
> I kept that silence, was labeled with behavior disorder and being emotionally disturbed, and given an IEP in the schools. Nobody was asking the important questions regarding safe touch, unsafe touch, safe secrets, and unsafe secrets. Yet I was being trained on tornado drills, bus drills, and fire drills.
>
> I knew how to run out of a burning building, but I didn't know how to tell secrets I was keeping as a young child. I moved at eight and a half years old, only to get that much closer to the next perpetrator in my life, a family member I loved and trusted.
>
> At eleven years old I woke up to my older teenage cousin with his hands down my pants. I will never forget that moment, trying to convince myself that it was all a bad dream and it really hadn't happened, but the

nightmare continued from ages eleven, twelve, and thirteen, during family gatherings, holidays, even while I babysat my little cousins. He threatened me that this was our little secret. He said, "No one will believe you. If you tell anybody, you will destroy this family. Erin, you have no proof."

So I stayed silent, and while I stayed in this silence, I kept my secrets locked away in a little childhood diary. I am going to read to you one thing I wrote in this little childhood diary just after being abused:

I sobbed the whole way home. A guy called Officer Friendly comes to school and teaches us not to answer the door when your parents are not home and don't talk to strangers. They don't teach us about people like my cousin Brian. I thought people like Brian jumped out of bushes and attacked you at night. They never warned us in school about our own family.

You see, we teach kids about stranger danger, yet 93 percent of the time children are sexually abused by someone they love and trust. Yet we focus so much on stranger danger in our society. In sixth grade I went through the DARE program. I graduated DARE, and, when you graduate, you've learned the eight ways to say no to drugs. But I stand here today and ask you, where were the eight ways on how to get away and how to tell today?

I decided to put away the shame and stigma and be a voice for those too afraid to come forward, the voice for those people you yourself know that have yet to speak up about the horrific crime that goes on day in and day out, that is going on right now in our own backyards and in our own communities. I decided to go after this law because we need to educate and empower kids through age-appropriate curriculum that will give kids the tools and knowledge about how to tell and keep their perpetrators from abusing them ever again. For example, take the Sandusky case. So many children could have been saved in that situation. We cannot leave this up to all the adults. Look at how many adults, from a coach, athletic director, and the president of the university, continued to allow this to go on for ten more years, allowing this man around children—ten years after it was brought to their attention.

I wish we could just leave it up to the adults, but we can't because we have adults that do not do the right thing. This is why we need to empower kids with their voice to tell, tell, tell, and to continue to tell until it stops. The kids end up being the heroes because they're saving another child's life from becoming the next victim from this evil, silent epidemic. I hope you'll see the importance in this and help me in making Michigan the fifth state to pass this as I go across this country on a mission to get this bill passed in all fifty states. I am determined and will not stop until all fifty states have passed this law, and I will get it done. Thank you.

Senator Proos stood and shared further:

Mr. Chairman, I think her testimony speaks loud and clear about the challenge that we face in our communities and our families and the need for us to address this silent epidemic, as she called it. Erin is one that managed to pick up the pieces, as you so rightly said, Mr. Chairman. She is making a positive out of what is a horrific negative to her, to our families, and to all who are impacted by this in the community. The difference here is she's trying to make a difference, and she's to be commended for that. It is an incredibly destructive and damaging sort of situation when one in four girls and one in six boys are victims of sexual abuse by the time they are eighteen years old. The numbers are staggering, and it's important that we as a legislature put together the right public policy with my colleagues and with you, Mr. Chairman, to make sure that we put an end to this.

After being commended for my courage to speak up and be a voice for children, the Health Policy Committee all voted in support of Erin's Law 37–0. It was now referred to the Michigan House of Representatives. Afterward, I spoke with several reporters who had many questions for me about the law, including the Associated Press. Governor Snyder agreed to meet with Senator Proos and me in his office at 2:30 PM. I briefly shared my experience and, more important, what Erin's Law is all about. It was great to meet with him, and he showed support for the law.

After testifying in Michigan, it was on to the next state. In September 2012, I flew to the capital of Pennsylvania. Pennsylvania had been in the spotlight because of the scandal at Penn State with assistant football coach Jerry Sandusky. What happened at Penn State was an example of why we need to empower children with their voice.

A grad assistant witnessed a child being abused in the shower by assistant coach Jerry Sandusky, and he went to head coach Joe Paterno and told him about it. Paterno stated he went to the athletic director and the president of the university, Graham Spanier, with the information when it occurred back in 1998. These men either witnessed or heard that a child was abused at the hands of Jerry Sandusky. They continued to witness Jerry Sandusky around children for the next decade. Because they failed to report Jerry Sandusky to police, ten more children from 2001–11 were sexually abused—ten more innocent children who could have been saved from a horrific crime but instead had their innocence killed and trust taken because grown adults failed to take legal and moral action.

There is no excuse for ex-president Graham Spanier, ex-vice president Gary Schultz, athletic director Tim Curley, and head coach Joe Paterno for covering up Jerry Sandusky's actions, and they should all be ashamed of themselves. These men concealed Sandusky's crimes and continued to allow a dangerous man to be around children. They showed a complete lack of empathy and well-being for children. I know ten-year-olds that would do the right thing, and yet we have grown men of high authority who covered it up to protect the university's image? That is sick, just sick and selfish! I am happy that every single one of them lost their jobs for their foolish, unethical decision to protect the school's football program. I guess we know where their priorities are—and one of them certainly wasn't protecting children from a child molester.

In June 2012, Jerry Sandusky was convicted of sexually abusing ten boys and found guilty on forty-five counts. He was sentenced in October to thirty to sixty years in prison. He was sent to a prison in Pennsylvania where most of Pennsylvania death row inmates are, which is right where he belongs.

Had the victims of Jerry Sandusky been educated in school not to stay silent to his threats and the gifts he gave them, I am confident they would have spoken up the first time. Aaron Fisher, the teen who as Victim 1 in the case reluctantly but resolutely blew the whistle that stopped Jerry Sandusky, released this statement: "Revealing I was the victim of sexual abuse was the most difficult task in my life. People ask me what could have made it easier for me and others in my situation. I tell them I wish Erin's Law, the legislation Erin Merryn is campaigning for state by state, was already established. Her proposed legislation calls for mandatory education about sexual abuse in elementary schools. Children are victimized and must be armed with protective information and taught to bring up the issue if they know of abuse attempts or abuse."

I flew to Harrisburg, Pennsylvania, in September 2012 to testify at the capitol on Erin's Law and to meet with Representative Gingrich, who had heard me speak a year and a half earlier in Pennsylvania at a child abuse conference. I reached out to her after the Penn State scandal, and she agreed it was time to introduce this bill.

The day began with a great press conference that morning. Representative Gingrich started the press conference off, then the chairman and cochairman expressed their support of Erin's Law. A former linebacker for the NFL, Al Chesley, then testified. It was very powerful seeing and hearing this big, muscular linebacker breaking down as he testified.

As a thirteen-year-old, I was sexually abused by a Washington, D.C., policeman. He was a neighbor whom I had revered. All of us kids in the neighborhood looked up to him. In an instant, my innocence was stripped from me. Replacing my innocence has been a lifetime of pain, fear, and paranoia. It was my first sexual experience. I was too frightened and confused to tell my mother and father about it. Somehow, in my thirteen-year-old mind, I believed this was my fault. The man that committed the sex crime against me told me to not tell anyone about it. My life became a living hell. I know the rape led to many dysfunctional areas in my life and [it took] all these years to talk about it. It still is painful, but I am speaking out in hopes that I might help protect other children from going through what I went through. That is why I am asking you all to support the child exploitation bill 2813.

I spoke at the press conference and told them the importance of Erin's Law and the crusade I am on in getting this law passed in all fifty states. My closing remarks went as follows: "In the end, this curriculum teaches kids how to tell, protecting them before they are abused, and will end up saving millions of children because, as we know, these sexual predators do not stop after one child. They will get as many kids as they can possibly get until they are caught."

The House Education Committee passed Erin's Law; however, time ran out to get it through before the session was up, just like in New York. It was reintroduced in January 2013 as HB19, where it passed in the House in February. It is currently waiting to be voted on in the Senate. Hopefully, it will be one of the many states to pass it in 2013, ensuring no other child will stay silent about a man like Jerry Sandusky.

Chapter
20

Woman of
the Year

**YOU MUST BE THE CHANGE YOU
WANT TO SEE IN THE WORLD.**

—Gandhi

O n Thursday, October 4, 2012, I received an e-mail from editor
in chief of *Glamour* magazine. This is what it said:

Hi Erin,

Hope you're well! I'll get right to the point: *Glamour* would love to
honor you as a Woman of the Year this fall. I've been so impressed
at the way your work has gained traction, and at your continuing optimism and powerful message. And in this year of Sandusky headlines,
you're such a bright spot. I hope you'll let us celebrate you!

Our event is the evening of November 12 at Carnegie Hall in New
York City. You'd be in incredible company. We have everyone from
Supreme Court justices to Oscar winners to Olympic gold medalists
with us. And we'd send a photographer to shoot you for the magazine
within the next few days.

Best,

Cindi

I couldn't believe what I had just read. I never went after Erin's Law
for recognition. I did it because I care about kids, and now I learned
that *Glamour* magazine wanted to honor me as a Woman of the Year
at Carnegie Hall. People dream of being onstage at Carnegie Hall, and
now I was about to be honored there. I said over and over to myself,
*I am no one special. I'm just a woman from the suburbs of Chicago who
wants to protect kids from the pain I suffered as a child.*

My family was so excited with this news. I was told I could only
tell my immediate family and boyfriend, David. They did not want

their top ten Women of the Year being made public until the magazine came out.

The same day I received this news, David and I were driving six and a half hours to his hometown in the suburbs of Columbus, Ohio. The entire drive down, I was on the phone with so many people from *Glamour* magazine—the writer doing the story, the photographer who was going to shoot photos the next day in Columbus, a producer to do a video piece for the night at Carnegie Hall, wardrobe to get my size to dress me for the photo shoot. It was all so surreal. I couldn't believe I was going to be recognized for this. What an honor it truly was.

I was told to think of anyone in the world I would want to present me with my award the night of the event. I was literally being told to pick any celebrity, singer, or politician to present to me. It was incredible. I started listing off people.

The next day David dropped me off at a hotel where I met with the makeup artist, wardrobe team, and photographers. When I arrived, there were the most beautiful flowers I had ever received from editor in chief Cindi Levi. After getting my makeup and hair done and being dressed in an outfit they had brought, we headed out to take pictures by the Scioto River in Columbus, Ohio. We were there for several hours. They were a great group of people, and they took more than nine hundred photos. The photo they used for the magazine is the one on the cover of this book.

When I was done, I was on the phone for nearly two hours with the writer who was writing my story for the magazine. I would be on the phone with her and an editor for the next week, making sure all the details and facts were correct.

The following week, a producer and camera crew from *Glamour* came out to my house to interview me and my younger sister on my being *Glamour* Woman of the Year. I told my story and then talked about my mission with Erin's Law. My sister spoke about what I am doing and how I have helped her.

Glamour magazine hit newsstands November 1. Selena Gomez was on the cover. She was also a Woman of the Year. Ethel and Rory Kennedy and Olympic gold medalists Gabby Douglas (gymnastics), Missy Franklin (swimming), Kayla Harrison (judo), Allyson Felix (track and field), and Carli Lloyd (soccer) were also honored. Supreme Court Justice Ruth Bader Ginsburg, photographer Annie Leibovitz, architect Zaha Hadid, Pakistan activist Sharmeen Obaid-Chinoy, actress and director Lena Dunman, and executive president of J. Crew Jenna Lyons were all Women of the Year with me. Each Woman of the Year was given a different title in the magazine. The title I was given was "Erin Merryn: The Guardian Angel." The article started off with a quote from Katie Couric. "Erin Merryn is a Woman of the Year because . . . She's taken her personal crusade and turned it into a public one. So many children will be protected because of her."

David and I arrived in New York City on a separate flight from my family. They arrived before us, and we had plans to meet up after we checked into our hotel rooms. As our van pulled up to the hotel, I opened the door and got out. Before I could even take a step, a male teen came running up to me in excitement.

"She is here! You are amazing. I am so excited to meet you. I admire you so much. Can I please have your autograph? Please, sign my magazine." He had *Glamour* magazine opened up to the page I was on. I noticed my dad, mom, and sister standing by the doors of the hotel. I knew they had put him up to this. Well, because the teen was so excited and made so much commotion, the paparazzi, who had been waiting for Selena Gomez, came running over and started snapping photos of me like I was someone famous. They were asking who I was. I was extremely embarrassed. My mom and sister were laughing so hard. They were enjoying every moment of it. They didn't really think the teen would do it when my mother asked him to. They got me good. And yes, I did sign the magazine, even though he was really waiting for Selena Gomez to show up.

That leads up to the magnificent day in New York City at Carnegie Hall. I began the morning with a rehearsal at Carnegie Hall, where I practiced where I would walk and what microphone I would speak into. Back at the hotel, a stylist brought dresses for me to try on until we found just the right one that I just loved. The one I had originally picked out was too large once I tried it on.

At 4:00 PM, I went down to the hotel room to get my hair and makeup done. When I arrived, the Olympic gold medalists were in the room. It was so surreal. All these women who I had watched just months earlier in the summer Olympics were now in the same room as me. I was being honored among women who wowed America over the summer, bringing home gold, and here I was. For the next hour, I sat there quietly, listening to them all talk and taking it all in, and then I got to talk to several of them. The hard work they put into their sport takes incredible talent to do what they did. I remember sitting there as a makeup artist was doing my makeup and hair and thinking back to what I wrote in my journal ten years earlier, the night I found out I had a learning disability: *I wish I could see where I will be ten years from now.* I could have never imagined it would be where I was.

My parents, sister, and David were all with me on this special night. My editor from my second book was meeting us at the event. My family arrived and took their seats once the doors opened. A car was sent to pick up David and me.

When we arrived at Carnegie Hall, there was a bunch of paparazzi waiting outside. As we walked in, I met the assistant who would be working with me throughout the night, directing me where to go and when. Julianna Margulies, who was presenting me with the *Glamour* Woman of the Year award, was waiting for the elevator as we walked in. Known best for her years on *ER*, she currently stars on *The Good Wife*.

I was led to the red carpet, where there were easily twenty or more photographers and videographers. As I walked the carpet, all the photographers were shouting my name. "Erin, here, over here, step back, look back, Erin, to your right, to your left, Erin, right in front of you, look back, Erin." *Ahh*—I didn't know who to listen to, and all I could see were dozens of white flashes. I was so out of my element. When I got to the end of the red carpet, I then spoke on camera. When I finished, David and the assistant were on the other side. Wow, that was something else! I never imagined I would walk a red carpet. That was for celebrities, and I certainly wasn't one of those.

We were led to a green room where all the other Women of the Year began arriving after walking the red carpet. There were several security people up there for Supreme Court Justice Ruth Bader Ginsburg. Soon, the night was about to begin. There were three large screens onstage flashing the images of all the Women of the Year as we walked in. We were led to our seats where I met up with my family and met my editor, Michele, for the first time. It was wonderful to meet her after so many phone calls and her doing such a wonderful job editing my second book, *Living for Today*.

We walked around talking to many celebrities and taking photos. Ethan Hawke was seated directly in front of me, and directly in front of Ethan was Mary J. Blige. Soon we were asked to take our seats, and the room of three thousand people quieted as the event began.

I was the second woman to be recognized that night as Julianna Margulies was introduced onstage. She said, "Look both ways when crossing the street. Always eat your green beans. Don't eat yellow snow. These were things my parents taught me when I was a child. Well, I will pass these things on to my four-year-old son, but I have lots more to add these days, too. In a time when child abuse has become a crisis, we must also teach our kids how to speak up when something goes terribly wrong. I am here tonight to introduce a woman who is giving kids that kind of know-how so they won't have to go through what she did. Erin Merryn is an outspoken survivor of childhood sexual abuse who says nothing will stop her from protecting our children. As a mother, I am so grateful. As a woman, I am so impressed."

The interview I did at home then played on the big screen. It showed videos and pictures of me testifying across the country and me talking about what happened and my mission to never give up. The video ended and Julianna introduced me.

"Ladies and gentlemen, I am proud to present Erin Merryn, *Glamour* Woman of the Year."

I took the stage and hugged Julianna, who handed me my award. I got a standing ovation, and the audience cheered as I stared out at three thousand people from the stage of Carnegie Hall. They clapped, cheered, and whistled for several seconds. That moment was a priceless one I will forever treasure. Standing there on a stage people dream of standing on, I was being recognized for my mission of protecting children from abuse.

In that moment, staring at thousands of people as bright stage lights shined on me, I thought of the dark world I had once lived in all alone, carrying painful secrets locked away in a childhood diary for so many years. I never imagined I would be standing on Carnegie Hall stage one day with three thousand people hearing my story—a story I once was too ashamed to share because my perpetrators had threatened me not to tell anyone. This is what I shared:

Thank you! I want to start off by saying thank you, *Glamour* and Cindi. You are going to help me save thousands of children tonight, because I know every single soul in this room will not want to walk out of here not wanting to help children from abuse. I guarantee every single person in this room, even if you feel this issue is not related to you, even if you feel you cannot relate, every single one of you at some point in your life will know somebody who has been sexually abused! I urge every single one of you to help me in my crusade to help take this national.

I won't stop! I won't stop until I get this passed in all fifty states, and then I will take it international. These children live in our own backyards if we take a very good look, and right now we allow people like Jerry Sandusky to silence our children. We cannot allow that anymore. I ask all of you tonight, let it not be the last night you hear about Erin's Law. A lot of you have a lot of power to do something, and I ask you as you walk out of here tonight that you do that.

I thank my parents, all the legislators who have helped me so far to get this law passed, the future legislators who will, and to all who have followed my mission and continue to help me persevere. As I said, I won't give up, and I hope you will help me in my mission to accomplish this. Thank you and God bless!

As I made my way backstage with Julianna, Katie Couric was standing there with her arms out and gave me a big hug, stating that we must get me on her talk show. Then I saw Chelsea Clinton. Suddenly I found myself standing with a nationally recognized journalist, actress, and former president's daughter. We posed together for a picture. Chelsea gave me her card to get in touch about helping with Erin's Law. I said good-bye to Katie and Chelsea, and Julianna and I were led to the elevator. Julianna looked at me in the elevator and said, "Well, how does it feel? You just spoke on the stage of Carnegie Hall. People spend a lifetime dreaming about doing that."

"Surreal! I'm speechless! This is all so amazing!"

Julianna and I went to get pictures taken with the photographer, where I held up my award before we were led back to our seats to watch the rest of the night's Women of the Year. The entire night was unbelievable, and I couldn't believe I was living it, let alone being honored in it. The night closed with 2012 *American Idol* winner Phillip Phillips singing his hit song "Home."

Before getting into the SUV to take us all to the VIP dinner held for the Women of the Year and their guests, a senator from Connecticut who was at the event approached me. "I want to introduce Erin's Law to Connecticut. Will you come testify?" she asked.

"Of course I will," I said.

I was thrilled. She gave me her card and asked me to call her when I returned home.

Once at the private VIP dinner, Tyra Banks walked up to our table.

"You are doing amazing things. I was reading your book on the ride over here that we got in our gift bags. Powerful story you have." My mom, sister, and I then posed for pictures with Tyra. We couldn't believe how tall she is. She towered over us. We then talked to Ethan Hawke and told him how much we loved his role in the movie *Alive*, based on the book I did my speech on in high school.

Midway through dinner, Olympic gold medalist Kayla came up to me. "Oh my God. I love what you are doing. I had no idea when I was getting my hair and makeup done with you what you were doing with your life. Can I please get your contact info before the night is over? I want to help you with Erin's Law."

Seated next to us at dinner were the Kennedys. The Kennedys called me over to their table. "Take a seat. What you are doing is just incredible."

I spoke more about my mission with them. They told me about what they were doing with their foundation and wanted me to be involved to bring awareness to Erin's Law for the students they reach around the world. I was thrilled. Ethel Kennedy hugged me and told me I was doing good things and not to stop. She was so sweet. I then posed for a picture with her and the Kennedy sisters.

I met so many incredible people that night, from the Women of the Year to the celebrities. I was honored on a stage I could never have imagined stepping foot on. It truly was an incredible night. We walked out that night talking with Olympic gymnast Gabby Douglas and her mom. Not far from my mind on a night of celebration in New York City were the children across the world who were going to bed that night with the same secrets I had kept as a child. They are who I will never give up fighting for. All my little brothers and sisters in Christ who I hold close to my heart. The clock doesn't stop. Children are hurting. They need a voice, and I won't stop fighting to ensure they all have one. It is a voice I never had.

There was work to be done on Erin's Law in both Michigan and Illinois before the year ended. As soon as I returned from New York, I was right back in the swing of things to pass Erin's Law.

The excitement in the fall of 2012 wasn't over. Two weeks after returning from *Glamour's* Women of the Year awards, I was in Columbus, Ohio, for Thanksgiving with David's family. On Black Friday, while millions were out trying to get a great deal on holiday gifts, I was about to receive the best gift I could ask for. While walking across Ohio State campus, where David graduated from, he got down on one knee and asked me to marry him. With tears of happiness streaming down my face, I said "yes." I had always feared I would spend my life alone because I didn't trust men after all that had happened to me. But I was wrong. I found one that I did trust, and I can't wait to spend the rest of my life with him. We were married on August 10, 2013, in a beautiful ceremony in Lake Geneva, Wisconsin. I can't wait to turn the page to start this new chapter of my life as a wife.

Chapter 21

The Miracle in Michigan

THE GREATER THE OBSTACLE, THE MORE GLORY IN OVERCOMING IT.

—Molière

After testifying in Michigan in the summer of 2012, where Erin's Law was passed through the Senate Education Committee, the bill was sent on to the House Education Committee, where it was stuck because so many other bills had been presented during the lame-duck session in November and December. A woman who worked for Michigan governor Snyder had heard I was at the capitol and had seen me on *Oprah*. She called her good friend Beckie, who was Oakland University women's basketball coach in Rochester, Michigan. Her husband was also the president of the university at the time.

Beckie was inspired by my courage and called me immediately the next day after I testified. She wanted to help with Erin's Law in any way she could for Michigan and the country. Inspired by how I carried no shame and went public, Beckie made the brave and courageous decision to go public with her own story. The national media picked up on the story after Beckie brought me to speak at Oakland University in October. A story ran in *USA Today* entitled "Oakland Coach Breaks Silence about Sexual Abuse." ESPN covered her coming forward among more than two hundred papers across the country. It was just another example of letting go of the shame and being a face and voice for millions, and I was so proud of her because I know it is not easy.

On November 8, Senator Proos met with the House majority floor leader to ask if it would be possible to schedule action on the bill as soon as the bill passed committee, and, if not, would he be willing to consider taking the bill up during the lame-duck session without a hearing in committee.

The Speaker of the House and the majority leader of the Senate agreed to meet for only nine sessions just days prior to the end of the legislative calendar for the year. The lame-duck session began November 27 with nearly one thousand personal legislative priorities on the calendar, including Erin's Law, and was expected to close on December 13. Any of the bills that failed to make it to final passage would die for the term and would need to be reintroduced in the new legislative session. That was the last thing we wanted to happen.

The House Education Committee chairman agreed to hold a hearing on Thursday, December 6, 2012. Senators Proos, Warren, and Emmons, having just completed the Senate session, arrived at the House Education Committee in time to testify in support of the bills. Following the presentation by the senators, Beckie testified with a halftime speech that captivated the members of the committee. All three bills were on Erin's Law, covering different aspects of the law. All four gave powerful and important testimony.

Erin's Law was reported from the House Education Committee with unanimous support and two abstentions from members of the Democratic minority. Senator Proos and his staff continued to insist that the bills be added to the schedule for final passage as soon as possible and learned that the floor leader might not be interested in scheduling the bills.

Now it was in the hands of the House to vote on. There was nothing on the House agenda the last week of the lame-duck session, which meant that what happened in Pennsylvania and New York might also happen in Michigan. We didn't want to start over, but time was against us. Senator Proos worked tirelessly to get it on the agenda. Beckie agreed to drive up again and speak directly to House members. Senator Proos said it was worth a try. At that point, anything was worth trying to get it heard and passed. Senator Proos and his staff prepared a two-page document that outlined the provisions of Erin's Law for all of the House members, and asked for support.

Senator Proos hand-delivered many of the memos to the members of the House on Wednesday evening while on the floor of the House of Representatives. Senator Proos formally asked Governor Snyder and his staff to assist in encouraging the House leadership to schedule a vote before the calendar was too full.

Thursday, December 13, was the final day Erin's Law could be voted on. Senators Proos, Warren, Emmors and other lobbyists were told over and over that there were just too many bills to get through and this wasn't a priority. Protecting children should be at the top of their priority. Senator Proos spoke directly with the chief of staff to the Speaker of the House and learned that the vote would not be scheduled.

Around 4:00 PM efforts to bring up Erin's Law for a vote continued despite the late hour and the hundred or more votes left to be cast on unrelated bills. Senator Proos and Coach Francis met again to discuss the progress and learned that the chief of staff to the Speaker and now the Speaker himself were not going to schedule the vote, as some in the Republican caucus were "uncomfortable" with adding additional requirements to schools, especially in the area of sexual abuse.

Finally, around 9:00 PM, Beckie made a final plea to Suzanne, chief of staff for the House: "Please, do not make Erin and me come back and testify again. It is too hard. Please take it up for a vote." When Suzanne agreed, Beckie literally picked her up off the floor and swung her around in excitement.

Senator Proos was told they were willing to schedule the vote if he was able to secure, on paper, the names of sixty-eight members of the House who were willing to vote yes on the bills. Given the hundreds of bills that were being debated and voted on in both chambers, Senator Proos enlisted the support of Representative Al Pscholka (majority caucus chair for the Republican caucus) to personally ask the members of the House if they would vote for Erin's Law. By 9:00 PM

Representative Pscholka reported more than eighty votes for Erin's Law to the Speaker and also asked that the vote be placed on the agenda.

After a long day that took a lot of effort on many ends, Erin's Law passed the House of Representatives 108 to 2 at 12:50 AM. Senators Proos, Emmons, and Warren met with Beckie to celebrate the passage of Erin's Law. The meeting was emotional for each member of the team, who never let the possible failure of passing Erin's Law stand in the way of success—success for those who have not had a voice and for those who will know how to tell in the future.

At 2:30 AM, Erin's Law, as amended in the House of Representatives, passed the Michigan Senate 38–0 and was transmitted to the governor for his signature. Senator Proos sent a text message of congratulations to me for my courage, persistence, and willingness to make a difference in the lives of hundreds of thousands of kids now and in the future, in Michigan and beyond. Many called what they had pulled off that night "the miracle in Michigan." Senators, lobbyists, and supporters for Erin's Law were told three times that they would not vote on Erin's Law, and my amazing team fought hard for my law and would not take no for an answer.

On the final day, December 13, 2012, when Erin's Law passed in Michigan, it was a huge accomplishment. God had a hand in that. There were hundreds of bills that didn't get voted on that night, but, in my eyes, the most important bill did—protecting and educating the innocent children of Michigan.

Governor Snyder signed Erin's Law on January 9, 2013, making it the fifth state to pass it. I attended an event put on by Oakland University, where I was an honorary girls' basketball coach with then head coach Beckie. I got to meet the lobbyist, senators, representatives, and many other amazing supporters who all came out for the Child Abuse

Awareness Day. There was a big halftime event for recognizing us all for getting Erin's Law passed.

During a reception, Lieutenant Governor Brian Calley was there and spoke. In front of a packed room, he turned to me to thank me for my hard work on Erin's Law in Michigan and handed over a copy of the signed law, along with the pen Governor Snyder used to sign it into law. I was so moved by this and felt an overwhelming sense of accomplishment in yet another state. I felt so blessed to be in a room of thirty or more people who all played a part in passing Erin's Law in Michigan. Before I left that day, the Speaker of the House gave me his business card and said if there was anything he could do to get me in touch with other states not to hesitate to ask me. He wanted to help.

On the flight home from Michigan that night, I looked out the window and thanked God for the miracle he gave us in Michigan and told him I looked forward to the next forty-five miracles he would give us across America.

Chapter 22

The Passage of Erin's Law

AND IF YOU FAITHFULLY OBEY THE VOICE OF THE LORD YOUR GOD, BEING CAREFUL TO DO ALL HIS COMMANDMENTS THAT I COMMAND YOU TODAY, THE LORD YOUR GOD WILL SET YOU HIGH ABOVE ALL THE NATIONS OF THE EARTH. AND ALL THESE BLESSINGS SHALL COME UPON YOU AND OVERTAKE YOU, IF YOU OBEY THE VOICE OF THE LORD YOUR GOD.

—*Deuteronomy 28:1–2*

At the same time that I was closely watching the progress of Erin's Law in Michigan, I had my own work back in Illinois. It was time to get the most crucial piece of Erin's Law passed, and this came out of the task force report. After ten months of research and meetings with task force members, we made our recommendations to the governor in May 2012 in a twenty-page report.

The recommendations for Erin's Law task force report went as follows:

The Erin's Law Task Force Recommends:

- Child sexual abuse prevention education should be taught in grades pre-K through 12. "Best Practices" should be included in this instruction.

- Training for school administrators should be amended to include child sexual abuse as a selective strand under the Illinois Administrator Academy.

- Child sexual abuse training should be provided as a certified professional development unit (CPDU) for certified non-administrative school personnel.

The law written in Illinois was found in the Comprehensive Health Education Act, which states that children pre-K through twelfth grade would be given sexual abuse and assault prevention education. Now we just needed to get it passed. I had to head back to the capital on December 4 to testify to the House Education Committee. It was my third time testifying at my state capitol.

Testifying became routine for me. It wasn't difficult retelling my life story over and over again; it was always therapeutic. Once again, I drove the message home to representatives on why we need to educate children on this issue. After testifying, Representative Jerry Mitchell was grilled by other representatives for sponsoring a mandate, since during his entire career as a representative, he was always against unfunded mandates on schools. As one representative continued to give him a hard time, Representative Mitchell handled himself very well and explained the importance of this law and how this was the right thing to do for children.

Erin's Law passed through the House Education Committee. We were thrilled because we knew it wasn't going to be easy getting an unfunded mandate through. The following day, it went to the House floor, where Representative Mitchell experienced the same tough questions about never supporting unfunded mandates, and suddenly his last bill before retirement was a mandate. Once again, he pushed the point and the importance of this mandate to save children. The House floor passed with 97 voting in favor and 10 voting against it.

On January 2, 2013, I was driving once again to the capitol of Illinois for what I hoped would be the last time I ever had to testify to Illinois lawmakers on Erin's Law.

I was with several members of the Erin's Law task force, along with Senators Bivins and Collins, the sponsors of the bill. There were a lot of bills to hear that afternoon. After running nearly two hours behind, the Education Committee began. After two bills were heard, Erin's Law HB6193 was called.

"With me is one of the most courageous individuals victimized by a sexual predator, who looks at the passage of this law as giving voice to children. She has a powerful testimony to be heard, and I thank her for coming forward and sharing with us her horrendous story of turning pain into a purpose," Senator Collins said.

I gave a powerful testimony of the voice I didn't have as a child and the voice I want every child to have now. I then took questions. One senator on the committee was grilling me with questions. He asked for examples on what would be taught. He asked about the costs of it. I explained the programs we had that would incur no costs or minimal costs for educating children and the training entailed to certify our teachers and support staff to teach the children. I mentioned that we should never put a price tag on a child's life. He asked about parents' involvement, and I explained the follow-up that we would have them do at home to continue the conversation. I didn't have to think for a second about each question he asked. I had an answer immediately. If you were in the room, you would have thought I had the list of questions this senator was going to ask me, but I didn't.

"Teachers already have so much to do in a day that they say they don't have enough time to teach everything they are supposed to accomplish in a year and now we are going to tell them to do this," he said.

"Schools can give up an hour or two a year to educate children on protecting themselves from being sexually abused. I think giving up a recess or two is worth saving the innocence of a child. Time is against us. Children are waiting to break their silence and be saved," I retorted.

When I finished, the chairman of the committee asked the senator if he was done, then he turned to me and said, "What district do you reside in?

"Schaumburg," I said.

"Oh, okay. So I know where to be looking for your name."

Laughter broke out. He was indicating that I would run for Senate. He went on to tell me how articulate I was and how I answered every single question I was asked without having to stop and think. With that, they all voted in support of Erin's Law.

On January 3, Erin's Law went to the House floor where it was passed 51 to 1. We did it! We did it! We did it! I was thrilled. After a three-year fight testifying four times for mandated sexual abuse education in Illinois schools, children will begin to be taught in the 2013–14 school year in Illinois on sexual abuse prevention. Now we just waited on the governor's signature to make it official. So many thought getting this mandate through would be impossible. I heard so much doubt concerning it over the three years, but I knew all along it would get done. Even the sponsors on both sides who introduced it were very skeptical of getting the mandate through because it is often impossible to do. God told me three years earlier I would be doubted, but that I would get it done. Had he not come to me in the night so strongly and convinced me, I would have never quit my job and gone after it. I never gave up having hope. I knew in my heart it would happen.

Chapter 23

Victory in January

CHARACTER CANNOT BE
DEVELOPED IN EASE AND QUIET.
ONLY THROUGH EXPERIENCE OF
TRIAL AND SUFFERING CAN THE SOUL
BE STRENGTHENED, AMBITION
INSPIRED, AND SUCCESS ACHIEVED.
ALL THE WORLD IS FULL OF SUFFERING.
IT IS ALSO FULL OF OVERCOMING.

—*Helen Keller*

On the morning of January 24, 2013, I pulled into the parking lot of a familiar place. Nearly fifteen years earlier, I had pulled into this same parking lot with my mom and sister, filled with fear and confusion. I had walked into a place of uncertainty, afraid the people inside would not believe what had happened to me. This place was the same place where I had reclaimed my voice, the Children's Advocacy Center. The center was where I had truly known I was finally safe from ever being harmed again. As my younger sister and I walked up the entrance to the center, she turned to me and said, "Wow, I haven't been back here since I was a kid when we were in groups with the other girl survivors."

This time we were walking through these doors for a very good reason. Governor Quinn was signing Erin's Law there. I had asked if he would be willing to sign the law in the very same place where I had found my voice, thus now giving all children a voice.

As we opened the door, the familiar bells on the door rang to notify staff someone was there. The place looked exactly the same as it had nearly fifteen years earlier. Reporters were already arriving. Chairs were set up facing a podium. The Children's Advocacy Center and I had reached out to the Chicago media hoping to get coverage. We were impressed as the minutes passed, as more and more reporters flowed in from the news stations and set up cameras in the back. Board members, legislators who sponsored the bill, several mayors, law enforcement, the founder of the center, members of the Erin's Law task force, and people from the community came out to be a part of the bill signing.

In a room where I used to be with other girls at the center in a support group talking about our flashbacks, nightmares, trust issues, fears, anxiety, the shame we carried, and sharing our stories of trauma,

I was now back, shameless and unafraid to talk about what happened to me. I was about to stand before the media and talk about being a survivor who turned pain into a purpose to protect children from living in silence the way I did.

We were thrilled when every single Chicago station covered it: NBC, ABC, CBS, FOX, and WGN. It was incredible. The *Chicago Tribune, Daily Herald,* and the Associated Press came out, too. We could not be happier with the media turnout. The signing was going to make headlines.

The governor arrived a little after 10:30 AM. Task force members, board members, legislators, and I stood behind the podium as Governor Quinn walked up.

It was at Erin's request that we come to the Children's Advocacy Center. I really believe in the Children's Advocacy Centers, and I know Erin does, too. We need to support these excellent centers that really protect our children.

I think today is a historical day in our state. A law is going to be signed. We have a heroic, courageous survivor in Erin, who went down to Springfield four different times to testify before the legislators to get this law passed. It is a testament that one woman with courage can make a majority. We always have to remember that democracy is a gift from God to all of us, and all of us have a role to play in our democracy in the state of Illinois.

Erin is a perfect example of what one person can do to make a difference that will save and protect the lives of countless numbers of children and not just in our state, because the mission of this young woman is to make sure that our whole country knows how important it is to have children educated at a tender and early age to make sure they are protected from any kind of sexual abuse.

This is Erin's mission and this is our mission, and I wanted to come here today and say I want to help you with other governors across America. We have a National Governors Association meeting in late February in DC. You can come with me.

"Definitely! Definitely!" I said with excitement.

"Instead of having to go all over the country," he said.

"You will save me many, many years," I responded.

Governor Quinn continued, "This young woman is getting married this year. I was reading all about her marriage at the same time she is organizing a national movement to protect children. There is a passage in scripture that says if you save one life, you save the whole world, and that is what Erin is doing. This Illinois woman is not even thirty years old. In the course of preparing for her wedding, she is nonetheless writing books, organizing in the best traditions of Lincoln's democracy person by person, and that is why we are here today. We are going to sign this law. You inspire us, Erin. Why don't you step forward and say a few words."

I was fighting back from breaking down and crying. I felt that lump in my throat and tears filling my eyes at hearing the governor talk.

Thank you! I am going to try not to get choked up here after that. I can't thank you enough, but I didn't do this on my own. I don't want to be the only one recognized here. I have Senator Bivins here, who was the first to introduce this. I had an amazing task force that helped make the recommendations for Erin's Law, who worked tirelessly for ten months. Jerry Mitchell, Senator Collins, there are just so many people involved in making this happen. I would do it over and over and over again to protect the innocence of children.

As Governor Quinn said, this place, the Children's Advocacy Center, is the reason I am standing here today. This is the place I was brought when I was thirteen years old, terrified and scared. My abusers had told me that no one would believe me, that the abuse was "our little secret." I was afraid the people in here would think I was a liar and not believe my story. Instead, I walked out realizing I was safe, that what had happened wasn't my fault, and I reclaimed my voice. And now I have come back here to have this law signed and give children of Illinois a voice—a voice to speak up and tell if they have ever been sexually abused. Finally, a message to every sex offender out there: Do not touch a child, because they are going to speak up. Thank you!

"Well said!" Governor Quinn said.

Mark Parr, the director of the Children's Advocacy Center, spoke on the important role the center fulfills and how Erin's Law would help: "Each of us has a responsibility to listen and to act when we suspect that children may be victims of abuse. If nothing else, we get the message across as adults that we want to educate our children, but we also want to be responsible as adults to take action when we are concerned for the well-being of children," he said.

Representative Crespo also spoke: "It wasn't easy to pass Erin's Law, as it is an unfunded mandate. However, in the end, there was tremendous bipartisan support. More than half of the members on the state's elementary and secondary education committee said they knew a family member who had been sexually abused. It is a big issue. Today we are here because of Erin. It takes a special person like Erin to move something forward. We need that little engine to move something forward. We're very lucky that we had Erin advocating for this," he said. "So thank you so much, Erin."

Senator Bivins then stepped up to the podium.

Thank you, Governor Quinn, for being here. This is a very important bill. About three years ago, Chief Dan Langloss called me up and asked, "Can I bring this young lady? We want to talk to you about legislation." When he told me what it was about, I was skeptical because of the age and knew it wouldn't be an easy task. But my mind was changed immediately after listening to Erin's story. She is giving a voice to children who have sat in silence for years. This bill will prevent children from sitting in silence or being abused in the first place. I commend you, Erin, for all your work. You told me at the time that you would get this passed in every state. I was a little skeptical, but you now have made a strong believer in me that you will get the job done.

State Senator Collins sponsored the bill with Representative Mitchell. She said, "I was so proud that Illinois is taking a bold step not only to equip our children with the awareness of the threat of sexual abuse but also to give them the knowledge that they're innocent and their self-worth is worth our protection. I commend you, Erin, for turning pain into purpose."

We then turned it over to the press for questions.

"Erin, what made you decide to go after this law?" a reporter asked.

"Honestly, I got my master's in social work and was working full-time at a counseling agency. God spoke to me one night. He told me to quit my job and go after this law. I ignored him several times and thought people were going to think I was nuts to quit my job and go after a law, especially in an economy in which it is so difficult to find a job. He kept putting it on my heart, kept putting it on my heart, and he told me I would have doubters but I would get it done. And look where we are today." Applause broke out.

"My running mate here," Governor Quinn said, referring to me (laughter broke out), "is hard to turn down, and I happened to be at the inauguration with many governors last week. Whether you are a Democrat or Republican, we all understand, especially at this time in our country's history, how important it is to make sure our children are safe from sexual abuse. With those who are victims, we want to make sure we not only protect them but help them become survivors. Erin, maybe talk a little more about that. We want anyone who has been abused to become a survivor."

I shared, "So many survivors carry stigma and shame, blaming themselves like this was their fault. They ask themselves, *What did I do wrong?* By going public with my story and putting a face and voice on this, I want survivors out there—and I know there are survivors in this room—to realize they have nothing to be ashamed of. This wasn't their fault. End the stigma and taboo around this subject. You can reclaim your voice the way I have. My innocence was killed, my trust was taken, but I reclaimed my voice, and I want every survivor of sexual abuse to do the same."

A reporter then asked, "Erin, what difference would it have made for you if you had had this curriculum as a child?"

I said "I think the difference this would have made for me, being that six-year-old sexually abused for the very first time, had I been educated in kindergarten that this is inappropriate touching, I would have gone home after that sleepover where I was sexually abused for the first time and told my parents what had happened. Instead, I was told by the perpetrator that 'this is our secret, no one will believe you, and I will come get you in the night if you tell anyone.' This man, a year later, right before my seventh birthday, proceeded to rape me. He continued to sexually abuse me. Then when I was eleven, I woke up to my older cousin sexually abusing me. These men both told me the same things: 'This is our secret and no one will believe you if you tell.' I knew when a van pulled up to my lemonade stand and the man inside wanted me to take the change out of his hand that he was a stranger, and you don't talk to strangers. I had been educated as a child on strangers. Had I been educated as a child on sexual abuse, I would have told."

Governor Quinn continued, "We have the best person in America to carry this mission out, and I look forward to working with you this year. We want to make this year, 2013, a year of Erin's Law across America. We have just begun. We are in January and we have more months to go. We are going to work together all across America. Erin agreed to go to the National Governors Conference with me."

Hugging me, Governor Quinn said, "That voice you heard, Erin, that voice that told you to step forward and make a difference, keep listening to that voice. Keep following your faith. You're our hero and always will be."

Governor Quinn made his way over to the table to sign Erin's Law. Standing next to him, I watched him sign the law I had worked so hard for in Illinois, and he handed me the pen he signed it with. Governor Quinn stood up next to me and put his arm around me. I couldn't stop smiling. I could feel the tears filling my eyes, but, unlike when I was a child at the Children's Advocacy Center, these were tears of happiness. I was overcome with joy. It was so surreal.

"Well, Erin, this is your law and you made it possible, along with many other people of good faith across Illinois," Governor Quinn concluded.

I hugged him and was overcome with pure joy and happiness. In a place I had once come to so broken and scared, I broke my silence for the very first time and reclaimed my voice. Here I was, almost fifteen years later, bearing witness to a law being officially signed that would give children a voice. It brought my journey of healing full circle. I cannot describe in words how joyous this was for me.

Several reporters came to speak with me afterward. One of the reporters walked back down the hallway with us into the interview room where my sister and I had first broken our silence. I told her how, during my interview, I focused on the big mirror inset into the wall; we both had no idea that a detective was sitting behind it. Now a cameraman from the news was behind that mirror videotaping us describing to the reporter what that day was like at the center.

My sister talked about how the center made it very comfortable to talk about the abuse. "They let us choose the room we wanted to be interviewed in and where we wanted to sit. I decided to sit on the beanbags when talking to the therapist," she told the reporter. "Coming back here, it brought me back to that age, just thinking back to those memories with my sister and trying to process all the pain and everything. The signing today was so unbelievable, and it's so exciting that many kids will be saved because of this law," my sister told the reporter.

I am becoming a part of history because I didn't stop believing and did what I felt in my heart was what I was being led to do by God. That night, every news station was reporting on Governor Quinn signing Erin's Law, and on the front page of the paper in the morning was a photo of Governor Quinn hugging me with a headline that said, "Erin's Law: A Real Law Now. Governor Quinn signs law mandating sexual abuse education."

Something else happened that day that didn't hit me until my sister and I were leaving the center and talking about how incredible the whole signing was. I looked at her and said, "This is one of the best days of my life." Then it dawned on me what I was saying. It goes back to where this book began. I always dread the start of a new year because it starts with January. January has always been the most painful and difficult month of the year for me, especially the end of

January. Every January reminds me of being locked in a room, terrified, screaming, and being raped as a little girl. Twenty-one years later, I have a reason to celebrate in January—the day Illinois children were given the voice I didn't have as a kid. I know God planned this according to his purpose.

 handsome

And we know that for those who
love God all things work together for good,
for those who are called according
to his purpose.

—Romans 8:28 (English Standard Version)

Afterword

In February 2013, Governor Quinn invited me to stay the night in the 158-year-old Governor's Mansion. That night, I slept on the bed of former president Abraham Lincoln, which was pretty amazing. Not very many people can say that. The next day Governor Quinn gave his yearly State of the State Address, where he recognized me before everyone for my work in passing Erin's Law.

A week later, I was extended another amazing invitation. I received a call that President Obama was going to be speaking in Chicago. Governor Quinn had two tickets and wanted me to be his guest of honor and have the opportunity to meet Mr. Obama. I was speechless and so grateful for all Governor Quinn's support.

On February 15th I had a front row seat to President Obama's speech on all the gun violence in Chicago. When it was over, he went around and shook hands with the guests. Since I was right up front, I had the incredible opportunity to meet him—and also got fifteen seconds to get across Erin's Law with the hope that he would help me get it into every state. I told him this was not the last time we would meet, and that I would not give up until Erin's Law was passed in all fifty states. He responded, "That is the attitude to have!"

On Friday, March 29, 2013, I sat down at the capitol in front of the Aging, Children, and Youth Committee in Arkansas and testified on Erin's Law. Governor Quinn introduced me: Representative John Baine. "Today I brought a special witness who I would like to introduce, Erin Merryn. We are introducing HB1988. It has been known as Erin's Law nationwide and five states have passed it with ten additional states introducing it. We are actually looking at phase one as an evaluation by which we are going to create a task force to look at ways we can combat child sexual abuse. With this, I would like to turn it over to Ms. Erin Merryn, who will be more than happy and capable to talk about this subject than I would ever be."

I addressed the committee, as I had others before: "I come here today from Chicago to speak on a very important topic that is near and dear to my heart, a topic I am very passionate about." As I spoke, I made eye contact with each representative listening to me testify.

One in four girls and one in six boys will be sexually abused before their eighteenth birthday. There are currently 42 million survivors of sexual abuse in America alone. Three million of those are children. We are just talking about America. Those 3 million kids could fill forty-six national football stadiums. As I often tell people, these children are sitting in our classrooms. Yet we don't understand or see the warning signs that are there. We often label these kids with behavior disorders and say they are emotionally disturbed, but we never get to the root of the problem. We give them aids, we hold them back, and we put all these resources into these children, but we are often failing these kids because we are not educating them. We are not giving them a voice and empowering them to speak up and tell if someone is ever doing anything inappropriate to them.

When I was just a little six-year-old, I met my best friend in school. Her name was Ashley. Ashley and I began doing everything together, and it was at Ashley's house I had my first sleepover. I was so excited as that little six-year-old going off to my best friend's house. I fell asleep that night only to wake up to her uncle coming into the room and sexually abusing me for the first time. This man went on to sexually abuse me many more times in my childhood. I didn't go home and tell my parents the next day what he had done. No, I stayed silent because the only message I was getting as a child was from my perpetrator: "This is our little secret. I will come get you, Erin. I know where you live. If you tell anyone, nobody will believe you." I was being brainwashed with this so I continued to stay silent. At seven years old, this man raped me. I can remember that day as if it happened yesterday. This man continued to sexually abuse me until I was eight years old. Finally, my saving grace came. We moved. But moving only got me that much closer to my next abuser. It wasn't that stranger danger I was taught about every year, "Don't go look for the lost puppy, don't talk to strangers," or, as I wrote in my childhood diary after being abused, *I sobbed the whole way home. A guy called Officer Friendly comes to school and teaches us not to answer the door when your parents are not home and don't talk to strangers. They don't teach us about people like my cousin Brian. I thought people like Brian jumped out of bushes and attacked you at night. They never warned us in school about our own family.*

You see, from ages eleven to thirteen, an older cousin was sexually abusing me. Once again, the only message I was given was, "This is our secret, Erin. If you tell, nobody will believe you." I knew as a child how to duck and cover from a tornado, how to run out of a burning building, how to evacuate a school bus, how to tell a teacher if I was being picked on and bullied by another student, and now we teach kids Internet safety, but we fail to teach kids on the prevention of sexual abuse, on empowering them if someone is abusing them, to speak up and tell a safe adult. You tell a parent, a teacher, a school social worker, a family member, somebody, but you don't keep this a secret.

I pulled out my DARE card that I had received in sixth grade when I graduated the DARE program. I lifted it up for all of them to see.

I was also taught DARE. We teach this across this country. I am sure we teach it right here in Arkansas. You see, DARE teaches us the eight ways to say no to drugs, but I ask you today, where are the eight ways on how to get away and tell today? They never came in my childhood, and as I mentioned, the only message that I got was, "This is our little secret. Nobody will believe you. I will come hurt you."

How did I finally find my voice? Well, unfortunately it was by learning that my little eleven-year-old sister was also being molested by this same relative. You see, these perpetrators live in our backyards. I guarantee every single one of you knows someone who has been sexually abused. We live in a society that looks the other way, pretends it isn't going on, when it is really in our faces all the time; we just fail to address it. There are people like Jerry Sandusky living in our own communities. They're out there. I want that little seven-year-old that is being sexually abused tonight to be educated on how to tell, through age-appropriate curriculum, on safe touch, unsafe touch, safe secrets, unsafe secrets, how to get away and tell today. So she will go to school tomorrow and report it. Because right now in our society that little seven-year-old will stay silent and continue to be abused by that stepfather, neighbor, or relative for years, and it isn't until she is thirty years old and in drug rehab that she finally comes to terms with what she never dealt with because she wasn't educated.

My goal here and across this nation is to get this law passed in every state. Every child deserves to be empowered with their voice and not to keep this a secret. Every child should know how to speak up and tell, the same way they know how not to talk to strangers or use drugs. I hope every single one of you hears the importance of this message. I say to all legislators across this country, the only ones that should be against this bill to help give kids a voice and educate our educators are the sexual offenders themselves. Thank you!

"Thank you for your powerful testimony. Representative Baine, do you have anything to add?" Chairman Meeks asked.

Representative Baine answered, "Just that I will be having the Department of Education talk about how they would staff such a force and the mechanics of it. I have talked to Dr. Kimble a lot about this, and they are very supportive. I want to thank our recent cosponsors. The state CASA association [Court Appointed Special Advocate Association] and the Arkansas Commission on Child Abuse, Rape, and Domestic Violence at UMAS [University of Arkansas for Medical Sciences] are to look at the public health aspects to take a broader view on this subject. We talk so much about child abuse, but this is the part that has always been taboo. It is time we break through this and have an honest conversation about this as adults and how we approach this with our children. We are not introducing curriculum today. Thank you very much, Chairman Meeks, and thank you, committee."

"Does anyone have any questions or comments?" Chairman Meeks asked. "Representative Scott, you are recognized."

"I would love to see you, sweetheart, in twenty years, because I just can't imagine what good things you are going to do with your life. Thank you so much for coming," she said.

"Thank you! I would like to say this law has been passed in five states and I have twelve more introducing it currently. I certainly hope we can make the sixth state Arkansas," I said.

"Anyone else on the committee have any questions or comments?" asked Chairman Meeks. "Representative Holcomb, you are recognized."

With a lump in his throat, you could hear him trying not to break down as he struggled to get the words out. "I just want to say, I do appreciate her testimony. It makes me want to cry. Thank you!" You could see his eyes filling with tears.

"Representative Harris, you are recognized."

"Thank you, Mr. Chair. Erin, I just want to say thank you, since we are here today and we are taking time, I am crying down here at the end of the table. My wife was a victim from five to thirteen from her own grandfather and she didn't ever tell a teacher because she didn't know how to. She thought she was protecting her cousin every summer. I thank you for doing this. I understand the importance. Also to Representative Baine, thank you for bringing this to our attention. I really appreciate it. Thank you for coming today."

"Are there any other questions from the members? Okay, with that," said Representative Baine, "we have more testimony from the Department of Education. We are going to go ahead and hold the bill at this point and hear the rest of it next Wednesday. We are going to go ahead at this time, and Aging and Youth is going to be adjourned. We hope everyone has a safe and happy Easter."

Before anyone could stand up, Representative Alexander put up his hand to stop the committee from leaving. "Representative Alexander," Chairman Meeks queried. "Does education have some opposition to it, or why do we have to wait on their testimony?"

"I am just doing what Representative Baine asked me to do," he said.

Representative Baine clarified, "They have no opposition. They want to come speak in favor of, but we scheduled a full hour on Friday on this. Because of the nature of the long weekend, I wanted to respect everyone's time. Erin couldn't come back next week and all my other speakers were able to reschedule to come testify next week. Their testimony is more about the mechanics of how we do it. I really wanted you to hear her testimony. I about broke down and cried the first time I heard her testimony, and I wanted to introduce her and give you a taste of what has been going on in my head the past two months since we started working on this bill."

"I will respect whatever you choose to do, but I would suggest if the only thing left to be done is to work out the mechanics, I am ready to do pass [pass the bill as currently introduced] right now," Representative Alexander said.

"I would be happy to accept your motion of do pass right now," Representative Baine replied.

"Okay, we have a little change of plans here. We will be that flexible. Before I accept the motion, I do want to go through the proper procedure here. Does anyone in the audience choose to speak for or against the bill? Seeing none, Representative Alexander, I will go ahead and accept your motion of do pass. All those in favor of passing House Bill 1988 say 'aye.'" The room filled with "ayes."

"All those opposed?" You couldn't hear a sound. "Congratulations, Representative Baine, you have passed your bill."

"Thank you, committee. I appreciate your kindness today. Have a wonderful Easter and hugs and kisses from this end of the table," Representative Baine said.

Less than three weeks later, on Tuesday, April 16, Arkansas went on to become the sixth state to pass Erin's Law. It was the fastest state to pass it. Afterward, I went on to testify in Nevada and Mississippi in the spring of 2013, where Erin's Law was also signed into law by the governors, making a total of eight states that have passed Erin's Law as of September 2013. As of September 2013 half of the country has either passed Erin's law or it has been introduced as a new bill to be voted on. With the governor's full support in helping me see out my mission of passing Erin's Law in all fifty states, I am confident we will get it done. I won't stop until we do, even if it takes me until I am being wheeled into the last capitol at ninety-five years old by my great grandchildren to testify. I have dedicated my life to this and will keep at it until I can say "mission accomplished."

After all that I endured and survived in my life, you might be wondering what the secret is behind my strength, courage, determination, ambition, perseverance, confidence, forgiveness, resilience, and attitude to never give up. The truth is, there is no secret. The answer lives within us all. It comes from our creator, God. When you have the Father, Son, and Holy Spirit in you, anything is possible. Some of us just have yet to discover, recognize, or believe it. The words are right there in my favorite passage from the Bible: "I can do all things through Christ who strengthens me" (Philippians 4:13).

My strength to never give up and do all that I set my mind to comes from the Lord. He is my constant source of guidance and is always reassuring me. He came to me in the night and told me what I was called to do in this life, showing me my purpose.

Whatever you are facing in life, I promise you, God hears you and loves you more than anyone else ever will. Go to him for guidance. Be patient, have faith, trust in Him, and in His time, he will answer. With faith, nothing will be impossible for you. I am living proof of that every day.

In May 2013, I stood on a stage in an auditorium to speak to middle and high school students in the small town of Scott City, Kansas, which has a population of less than 5,000 people. I shared my story with the students, then I talked about Erin's Law. You could hear a pin drop in the room, and all eyes were on me. I asked every student to raise his or her hand if they had done tornado drills, bus drills, fire drills, DARE, bully intervention, and Internet safety in school. Every single hand went up each time. Then I asked, "How many of you have learned about sexual abuse prevention in school; to speak up and tell if you have been sexually abused, not to keep it a secret, and that someone will believe you?" Not a single hand went up. I went on to explain to the students that this is what I was trying to change in our country, and how Erin's Law will give children the voice I never had. I told them it would make it a lot more difficult for sex offenders to keep children silenced.

I closed by telling the students, that if they are one of those who has had their voice silenced, today was the day to let that voice be heard. I told them to break their silence and reclaim their voice. I directed them to counselors in the audience who could talk with them after-wards if they needed help. Five children that day broke their silence for the first time after hearing me speak. These are students who might not otherwise come forward until much later in life, and would pos-sibly have suffered more years of abuse. This is just one tiny town in America and one example showing exactly why we need Erin's Law in every state for the millions of children out there living in silence.

I turned my pain into a purpose. I am doing my part to end this silent epidemic across this world by giving children a voice. Will you do your part? Or will you do what so many millions have been doing for centuries by closing this book and looking the other way, pretend-ing this isn't happening. The choice is yours.

Appendix

Warning Signs of an Abused Child

Behavioral Signs

- ✓ Inappropriate sexual knowledge
- ✓ Inappropriate sexual behavior
- ✓ Nightmares or bed-wetting
- ✓ Emotional outbursts
- ✓ Displays of anger and rage
- ✓ Extreme startle-response when touched or a certain person enters the room
- ✓ Suddenly doesn't want to be around a certain person
- ✓ Large weight fluctuations or changes in appetite
- ✓ Suicide attempts
- ✓ Suicidal ideation
- ✓ Self-harming
- ✓ Runs away
- ✓ Sudden changes in school performance, grades, or drops out

- ✓ Overly protective and concerned for siblings, assuming a caretaker role
- ✓ Post-traumatic stress disorder or rape trauma syndrome symptoms
- ✓ Extreme responsibility and safety-consciousness
- ✓ Criminal activity
- ✓ Wearing excessively loose-fitting clothing, or more layers of clothing than weather requires
- ✓ Dissociation (unresponsiveness, detachment, confusion, staring blankly, unexplained crying, feeling of separation from reality, feeling of floating, out-of-body experience, feeling that everyone but self is experiencing reality or vice versa)
- ✓ Panic attacks and/or anxiety
- ✓ Feeling of choking or suffocating
- ✓ Unexplained fear of water touching face (pool, shower, etc.)
- ✓ Feeling dirty, disgusting, and/or damaged
- ✓ Feelings of shame
- ✓ Fear of extreme loss of control; extreme need to feel in control
- ✓ Feelings of extreme vulnerability
- ✓ Constant anticipation of pain
- ✓ Anticipation of early death
- ✓ Extreme sensitivity and/or irritability
- ✓ Lack of confidence
- ✓ Feelings of worthlessness and/or lack of self-respect
- ✓ Intense fear of being wrong

Physical Signs

✓ Difficulty walking or sitting

✓ Bloody, torn, or stained underclothes

✓ Bleeding, bruises, or swelling in genital area

✓ Pain, itching, or burning in genital area

✓ Frequent urinary or yeast infections

✓ Sexually transmitted infections, especially if under fourteen years old

✓ Pregnancy

✓ Severe gag reflex, even with nothing in or near mouth

✓ Frequent or chronic severe nausea

✓ Chronic, unexplained pelvic pain

✓ Addiction

Darkness to Light's Seven Steps for Protecting Our Children

Step 1: Learn the Facts

One in four girls and one in six boys are sexually abused before their eighteenth birthday. Sixty percent of children are abused by someone the family trusts. Forty percent are abused by a family member. Fifty percent of victims of forcible sodomy, sexual assault with an object, and forcible fondling are under age twelve. Seventy percent of all sexual assaults reported occur to children seventeen and under.

Step 2: Minimize Opportunity

Abusers often become friendly with children, trying to gain trust and access to them alone. Think about the risks of one-adult/one-child situations. Think carefully about situations with older children having access to younger children.

Step 3: Talk About It

Teach your children about their bodies and what abuse is. Teach that it is against the rules for anyone to touch them inappropriately by teaching them what parts of their body nobody should be touching. Start early and talk often about sexual abuse. Be proactive. If a child seems uncomfortable with someone, talk about it with them.

Step 4: Stay Alert

Look for the physical, emotional, and behavior signs in a child being abused.

Step 5: Make a Plan

When a child discloses sexual abuse, believe the child. Praise them for telling and not keeping it a secret. Report it immediately to the police. It is required in all fifty states that if you work with children, you are a mandated reporter and must report the abuse. Some states require everyone to report.

Step 6: Act on Suspicions

Trust your instinct if you feel a child is being abused and report it today. Call Darkness to Light's Helpline at 1-866-FOR-LIGHT to be routed to resources in your community or call the Childhelp USA National Child Abuse Hotline at 1-800-4-A-CHILD. Children's Advocacy Centers coordinate all the professionals involved in a case. If you are unsure about whether to make an official report, contact a Children's Advocacy Center. You will be directed with the next steps. They can be reached at 1-800-239-9950.

Step 7: Get Involved

Donate your time and resources to help organizations like Prevention Programs, Children's Advocacy Centers, and Rape Crisis Centers. Use your voice to make your community safer for children. Write your members of Congress, demanding government to do more to protect children from sexual abuse. Support legislation that protects children such as Erin's Law.

Take action and talk to your kids. Don't wait until it is too late. Talk to your kids about sexual abuse. Once a predator gets your kids, they take their innocence and silence them, and it might be months, years, even decades before they tell you anything—all because nobody ever had the conversation with them on sexual abuse prevention.

Follow the steps below to ensure your kids know how to speak up and tell. Sit down with your children and talk about people they can trust and feel safe with. Help them write this list out. Explain to your kids that the conversation you are having with them isn't to scare them but to keep them safe from being hurt.

Talking Points for Parents

✓ Start the conversation. "While you should not talk to strangers, sometimes people we know that are not strangers can hurt us. This conversation is not to scare you but to keep you safe."

✓ Ask your kids to define safe touch. Establish a list with your kids that you feel are safe touches and a list of unsafe touches.

✓ Define unsafe touch. "The place your bathing suit covers is your private places that nobody should look at or touch." Go into detail about their private places and explain how somebody touching them there is not a safe touch, and, if someone tries to touch them that way, they need to get away and tell another adult (on their list of safe people) right away.

✓ Give examples. "The same way we would tell you to kick and scream if a stranger tried grabbing you, do the same if someone tries touching you."

✓ Define what a safe secret is. After they answer, give them an example of a safe secret: "Grandma's Surprise Sixtieth birthday, your brother's birthday gift," and so on.

✓ Define what an unsafe secret is. Explain to your children how someone who might try to touch them inappropriately will try to make them keep it a secret. Explain to them that this is an unsafe secret. For even younger children, a good place to have this conversation is when you are bathing them in the bathtub. Point out their private areas while talking about safe touch, unsafe touch, safe secrets, and unsafe secrets.

✓ Explain potential threats. "The person might try to use threats to keep you silent by saying they will hurt you if you tell anyone, that nobody will believe you." This is your chance to drill into your kid's heads that somebody will believe them and how important it is that they have to tell if anyone ever tries anything that makes them feel uncomfortable and unsafe.

✓ Revisit the list of safe people to talk to. Go back to the list they created of the people who are safe that they can talk to. Tell your children they can always come to you with anything, but that, if they do not feel comfortable telling you something, they can tell someone else. Don't take offense at this. Kids often want to protect their parents, or a predator might tell kids they will hurt Mommy or Daddy. A child might be afraid to tell Mommy, thinking she might get hurt and maybe the teacher or Grandma is the next person they feel safest sharing something with. Find a safe place in your children's room where they can keep their list of safe people they trust.

✓ Teach them to pass the message. Before ending the talk with your kids, ask them, "What if one of your friends came up to you tomorrow and told you they had a secret to tell you and they shared that someone was touching them in their private places but that they have to keep it a secret. What would you do?"

✓ Keep the conversation going. Finally, don't let this be the last time you talk to your kids about this. Keep the dialogue open. It keeps it fresh in their minds so that they have the knowledge to speak up and be safe.

Recommended Resources

Chelsea's Light Foundation is a 501(c)(3) nonprofit organization created after seventeen-year-old Chelsea King of California was raped and murdered by a convicted sex offender. This organization strives to unite and set free the power of engaged communities, protecting the innocence and joy of childhood and inspiring positive change. Their desire is to unite and lead people who are passionate about protecting children and inspiring positive change in their communities. Chelsea's Law was founded on the belief that violent sexual predators who go after children are a uniquely dangerous problem. Signed unanimously into law in September 2010 in California, it ensures that the state does everything it can to keep sex offenders who target children from engaging in even more atrocious crimes upon release, and that those who commit the worst violent sexual crimes against children are put away for life.

Chelsea's Light
12463 Rancho Bernardo Road, #519
San Diego, CA 92128
info@chelseaslight.org
www.chelseaslight.org

Darkness to Light is a nonprofit organization with a mission to diminish the incidence and impact of child sexual abuse so that more children will grow up healthy and whole. Their programs raise awareness of the prevalence and consequences of child sexual abuse by educating adults about the steps they can take to prevent, recognize, and react responsibly to the reality of child sexual abuse.

Darkness to Light
Suite 200
Charleston, SC 29403
843-965-5444
www.darkness2light.org

KlaasKids Foundation is a 501(c)(3) public charity organization devoted to preventing crimes against children, assisting in the recovery of missing children, giving proactive solutions for keeping children off missing posters, and lobbying for legislative action. KlaasKids Foundation was established in 1994 by Mark Klaas to give meaning to the death of his twelve-year-old kidnapped and murdered daughter Polly Hannah Klaas and to create a legacy in her name that would be protective of children for generations to come.

KlaasKids Foundation
P.O. Box 925
Sausalito, CA 94966
415-331-6867
info@klaaskids.org
www.klaaskids.org

Little Warriors is a charitable organization located in Canada with a national focus that educates adults about how to help prevent, recognize, and react responsibly to child sexual abuse. Little Warriors also provides information about the prevalence and frequency of child sexual abuse and information about healing and support resources. Little Warriors' vision is to build the first of its kind treatment center for children.

Little Warriors Be Brave Ranch
Little Warriors
328 Circle Square Professional Building
11808 St. Alberta Trail
Edmonton, AB, Canada T5L4G4
708-447-1343

National Children's Alliance is a nationwide not-for-profit membership organization whose mission is to promote and support communities in providing a coordinated investigation and comprehensive response to victims of severe child abuse. It is an organization with a vision that will have met success when every child has access to the services of an accredited Children's Advocacy Center.

National Children's Alliance

516 C Street, NE
Washington, DC 20002
800-239-9950 or 202-548-0090
www.nationalchildrensalliance.org/

National Center for Missing and Exploited Children (NCMEC) was established in 1984 and is the leading nonprofit organization in the United States. The center works with law enforcement, families, and the professionals who serve them on issues related to missing and sexually exploited children. As part of its congressional authorization, NCMEC has created a unique public and private partnership to build a coordinated, national response to the problem of missing and sexually exploited children, establish a missing children hotline, and serve as the national clearinghouse for information related to these issues. With help from corporate partners, they have circulated billions of photos of missing children, and their employees have assisted law enforcement in the recovery of more than 183,000 missing children. They have trained more than 300,000 law enforcement officers, prosecutors, and healthcare professionals at their Alexandria, Virginia, headquarters, branch offices, and online.

National Center for Missing and Exploited Children

Charles B. Wang International Children's Building
699 Prince Street
Alexandria, VA 22314-3175
To report information about a missing child call
1-800-THE-LOST (1-800-843-5678)
www.missingkids.com

National Center for Victims of Crime, established in 1985, is the nation's leading resource and advocacy organization for crime victims and those who serve them. For more than twenty-five years, the National Center has led this nation's struggle to provide crime victims with the rights, protections, and services they need to rebuild their lives.

National Center for Victims of Crime
2000 M Street NW, Suite 480
Washington, DC 20056
202-467-8700

National Sex Offender Registry: Dru Sjodin National Sex Offender Public Website (NSOPW) is an unprecedented public safety resource that provides the public with access to sex offender data nationwide. NSOPW is a partnership between the U.S. Department of Justice and state, territorial, and tribal governments, working together for the safety of adults and children. First established in 2005 as the National Sex Offender Public Registry (NSOPR), NSOPW was renamed by the Adam Walsh Child Protection and Safety Act of 2006 in honor of twenty-two-year-old college student Dru Sjodin of Grand Forks, North Dakota, a young woman who was kidnapped and murdered by a sex offender who was registered in Minnesota.

National Sex Offender Registry U.S. Department of Justice
950 Pennsylvania Avenue, NW
Washington, DC 20530-0001
www.nsopw.gov/

PAVE is a nonprofit organization that stands for Promoting Awareness Victim Empowerment. It uses social, educational, and legislative tactics to shatter the silence of sexual abuse. Founder Angela Rose was abducted at knifepoint at age seventeen from the parking lot of the mall where she worked and was assaulted by a repeat sex offender on parole

for murder. Instead of staying silent, Angela took a stand and worked
with survivors as well as the community to help enact Illinois's Sexual
Dangerous Persons Commitment Act in 1998.

PAVE
P.O. Box 26354
Alexandria, VA 22313
877-399-1346
info@shatteringthesilence.org
www.Pavingtheway.net

radKIDS is a Personal Empowerment Safety Education Program that
began in 1998. A not-for-profit educational organization dedicated to
providing realistic choices and options to children and parents concerning their overall safety in the world today. It is our mission to provide,
through education, realistic choices for children to avoid and/or escape
violence or harm in their daily lives.

radKIDS, Inc.
9 New Venture Drive Unit 4
South Dennis, MA 02660
508-760-2080
www.radkids.org

Rape, Abuse, and Incest National Network (RAINN) is the nation's
largest antisexual assault organization. RAINN operates the National
Sexual Assault Hotline, Online Hotline, and confidential services; educates the public about sexual assault; and leads national efforts to prevent
sexual assault, improving services to survivors and ensuring that rapists
are brought to justice.

Rape, Abuse, and Incest National Network (RAINN)
2000 L Street, NW
Suite 406

Washington, DC 20036
202-544-3064
Fax: 202-544-3556
info@rainn.org
www.rainn.org

Stop It Now! prevents the sexual abuse of children by mobilizing adults, families, and communities to take actions that protect children before they are harmed. They provide support, information, and resources to keep children safe and create healthier communities. Since 1992, they have identified, refined, and shared effective ways for individuals, families, and communities to act to prevent child sexual abuse *before* children are harmed—and to get help for everyone involved.

Stop It Now!
351 Pleasant Street, Suite B-319,
Northampton, MA 01060
413-587-3500
Helpline: 1-888-PREVENT

Prevention Programs

CAP: Child Abuse Prevention. Since its inception in 1985, CAP has trained more than 3 million children, parents, and teachers to prevent peer abuse or bullying, stranger abduction, and known adult assault. CAP seeks to integrate the best resources of a community in an effort to reduce a child or young person's vulnerability to any type of verbal, physical, and/or sexual abuse. New Jersey's CAP projects work closely with the local school districts, parent/teacher associations, homeschool groups, and other community groups. CAP has a threefold educational approach to child abuse prevention that includes training in the following areas: staff in service, parent programs, and individual classroom work-shops for children and teens. CAP's motto is to teach children to be "Safe, Strong, and Free."

CAP: Child Abuse Prevention
107 Gilbreth Parkway
Mullica Hill, NJ 08062
856-582-7000
njcap@eirc.org

Child Help: Speak Up Be Safe. Speak Up Be Safe is a research-based, comprehensive primary prevention education curriculum that equips children in grades 1–6 and their adult community with skills they need to play a significant role in the prevention or interruption of physical, emotional, and sexual abuse and neglect. The school-based curriculum utilizes web-based tools, focusing on building self-esteem and safety skills within the child to include addressing today's societal risks children encounter every day, such as Internet and cell phone safety. The curriculum redirects focus on the adult's responsibility and skill building by engaging the states, schools, facilitators, teachers, parents, and designated safe adults in the protection of our children. The program also focuses on meeting state standards for health and safety education, which allows a complementary curriculum-based approach to this growing epidemic.

Child Help: Speak Up Be Safe
15757 N 78th Street, Suite B
Scottsdale, AZ 85260
1-800-245-1527
www.speakupbesafe.org

Child Lures Prevention: Think First and Stay Safe. Child Lures' mission is to help ensure personal safety to children and youth through awareness, education, advocacy, and action. The Think First and Stay

Safe program strives for a balanced perspective that will preserve as much of the innocence and optimism of childhood as possible. While adults are primarily responsible for keeping kids safe, Think First and Stay Safe enables children to take an active role in protecting themselves when necessary. Schools provide an ideal environment for reaching every child with positive messages and prevention strategies empowering them with their voice.

Child Lures Prevention
5166 Shelburne Rd.
Shelburne, Vermont 05482
1-800-522-2197
www.childluresprevention.com

Committee for Children: Talk About Touching. The Talk About Touching program uses time-honored, developmentally appropriate teaching techniques to help children learn safety skills. These include refusing and reporting unsafe touches but also encompass basic safety skills (such as for cars, bikes, and fire) and the Always Ask First Rule. It's a great way to talk to young children about sensitive but essential topics and teaches children the ability to distinguish between safe and unsafe touches and develop the skills to say NO to unwanted touches.

Committee for Children
2815 Second Avenue
Suite 400
Seattle, WA 98121
1-800-634-4449
www.cfchildren.org

Kids in the Know and Commit to Kids (Canada) is a national researched-based interactive safety education program for increasing the personal safety of children and reducing their risk of sexual victimization by teaching children critical problem-solving skills. Designed for children from kindergarten to high school, it focuses on building self-esteem through teaching critical problem-solving skills. It teaches the following Seven Root Safety Strategies: (1) Shout NO! (2) Run (3) Tell Someone (4) Keep and Speak Secrets (5) Buddy System (6) Trust Your Instinct (7) Dignity and Respect. They also teach: "If asked to go and your parents don't know, shout NO! If asked to share and your parents aren't aware, say NO!" Commit to Kids program was created to help organizations create safe environments for children. The program includes policies, strategies, and step-by-step plans for reducing the risk of child sexual abuse within an organization, encouraging organizations to take an active role in protecting children in their care.

Canadian Centre for Children Protection Inc.
615 Academy Road
Winnipeg, Manitoba, CANADA R3N 0E7
204-945-5735
www.protectchildren.ca

Safe @ Last is a personal safety curriculum that empowers students in kindergarten through sixth grade by providing critical skills and tools to stay safe and avoid dangerous situations. Lessons cover safe and unsafe touch, safe and unsafe secrets, assertiveness, boundaries, Internet safety, bullying, and so much more. Each session builds on and reinforces the skills learned in previous sessions with opportunities for students to practice each learned skill. The program includes age-appropriate learning techniques such as role playing, music, puppets, games, stories, videos, and an interactive online workbook to enhance the learning process for each individual student.

Safe @ Last
101 French Landing Dr.
Nashville, TN 37228-1511
1-866-362-4406
615-259-9055
www.besafeatlast.com

Recommended Reading

Children's Books

The Birthday Suit by Kristina Muldoon

Fred the Fox Shouts No by Tatiana Y. Kisil Matthews

I Said NO! by Kimberly King

My Body Belongs to Me by Jill Starishevsky

My Body Is Private by Linda Girard

My Body Is Special and Belongs to Me by Sally Berenzweig and
    Cherie Benjoseph

The Right Touch by Jody Bergsma

Sara Sue Learns to Yell and Tell by Debi Pearl

Some Parts Are Not for Sharing by Julie Frederico

Some Secrets Should Never be Kept by Jayneen Sanders

Tell Somebody It Happened to Me by Nancy Flowers

The Swimsuit Lesson by Jon Holsten

Adult Books

Allies in Healing by Laura Davis

*The Body Remembers: The Psychophysiology of Trauma and Trauma
    Treatment* by Babette Rothschild

The Courage to Heal by Ellen Bass

The Courage to Heal Workbook by Laura Davis

*8 Keys to Safe Trauma Recovery: Take-Charge Strategies to Empower
    Your Healing* by Babette Rothschild

Living for Today by Erin Merryn

Lucky by Alice Sebold

Healing from Trauma by Jasmin Lee Cori

Hush by Nicole Bromley

The PTSD Workbook by Mary Beth Williams

The Sexual Healing Journey by Wendy Maltz

Silent No More by Aaron Fisher

Stolen Innocence by Erin Merryn

A Stolen Life by Jaycee Dugard